W9-AZX-990

PRAISE FOR *NUDGING CONVERSIONS*

"The splendor, beauty, and freedom of the Catholic faith is something our culture longs for. Joy and truth go a long way in a world that has tried everything yet feels empty. Carrie Gress shows us that the beauty of Catholicism often only needs to be nudged for those searching. God works through small and simple things and he wants to work through you to bring others closer to Him. *Nudging Conversions* is a must read for anyone who wants to joyfully share their Catholic faith in a culture seeking love in all the wrong places."

- Shawn Carney

Co-Founder of 40 Days for Life, and Co-Author of *40 Days for Life: Discover What God Has Done...Imagine What He Can Do*

"Dr. Gress urges us to realize that evangelization (bringing others to the love of Jesus Christ) doesn't happen in a vacuum. It takes real people of real faith to reach out to that hurting person in the coffee shop, that disenfranchised teenager in our own family. Recognizing the challenges we face today in putting our faith into action, Gress offers a real roadmap to take the reader from inspiration to practical application of the deposit of faith. *Nudging Conversions* offers suggestions which can make a tangible difference not only for the hopeful evangelist but for those engaged actively in ministry today."

- Dr. Christine A. Mugridge

Author of *Called by Name*, contributor to Relevant Radio, Immaculate Heart Radio/EWTN, research specialist on St. John Paul II's theology of communication.

"Carrie Gress has written a marvelous book, a book full of practical assistance, of wisdom, of love. No Christian is ever fully fulfilled until she brings others around her back into the arms of Christ. Bringing the gospel to others, especially those near us, is our vocation.... Millions of Catholics at Mass ache with passionate prayers that children, uncles, and close friends of theirs come 'back home' to a loving Father. Prayers storm heaven every day pleading for that to happen. But for God to act, WE have to be his gentle hand upon the back, speaking tongue, embracing arm. We have to give our dear ones a nudge. If each of the 45 million Catholic adults during their allotted years of life nudge even two of their dearest ones back to our Father, that would mean an immense increase in those rejoicing together again in the deepest of all loves. Carrie gives scores of practical tips on how to let the Lord give that nudge through you."

- *Michael Novak*

Author, philosopher, theologian, diplomat

"Rooted in the teachings of Popes Saint John Paul II, Benedict XVI, and Francis and drawing deeply on the riches of Scripture and Tradition, *Nudging Conversions* is practical and wise. It is also challenging, filled with direct exhortations and bracing insights into the heart of the Christian life and the essential nature of evangelization. This toolbox will help readers break out of the boxes of indifference and pride and build relationships marked by joy and grace."

- *Carl E. Olson*

Best-selling author and editor of *Catholic World Report*

"For all those who don't feel like they're equipped for the work of evangelizing, *Nudging Conversions* proves otherwise, offering practical, accessible guidance for how all of us can bring those we love closer to Christ through our daily prayers and ordinary interactions."

- *Emily Stimpson*

Author of *These Beautiful Bones*, *The Catholic Girl's Survival Guide for the Single Years*, and co-author of *The American Catholic Almanac*

nudging CONVERSIONS

A Practical Guide
to Bringing Those You Love
Back to the Church

CARRIE GRESS

Nudging Conversions

Published by Beacon Publishing

ISBN: 978-1-942611-23-3

For more information on this title and other books and CDs available through the Dynamic Catholic Book Program, please visit: www.DynamicCatholic.com

The Dynamic Catholic Institute
5081 Olympic Blvd.
Erlanger, Kentucky 41018
phone: 859-980-7900
email: info@DynamicCatholic.com

Designed by Shawna Navaro and Leah Nienas

Printed in the United States of America

Table of Contents

To Debbie Devereaux
and all the Rosary group:
Thank you for all your
gentle nudges.

INTRODUCTION

Since the pontificate of Pope John Paul II, there has been much discussion of the New Evangelization and a new springtime in the Catholic Church. The topic has generated a lot of interest, especially as new trends are being seen among the young, seminaries are filling up, and growing pockets of orthodoxy are emerging. These are all very good and important changes after decades of heterodoxy and dissent in the Church. Less attention, however, has been given to how these quiet but powerful changes are taking place from one person to the next.

The idea for this book was sparked after Mass one day when I started chatting with two elderly women who were comparing notes on how many children they had who had left the Church. Ninety-two-year-old Mary lamented that she had five daughters without faith. It got me thinking about what can be done to help bring those we love back into the fold.

Mary and her friend, sadly, are not alone. There isn't a Catholic who takes his faith seriously who doesn't have a parent, sibling, aunt or uncle, coworker, grandparent, child, neighbor, or friend who has left the Church or hasn't been able to find a way to it. Meanwhile, in every church, at every Mass, every day, people are praying for these parents, children, siblings, and loved ones to return to the Church. This book considers what we can do to help bring them home. Evangelization doesn't usually happen in a flash like it did for St. Paul, but instead, like the lighting of a candle, it passes slowly and quietly from one person to the next.

The reason for calling the book *Nudging Conversions* is the recognition that a conversion is a mysterious act of grace. There seems to be no exact science. A person who seems ripe for conversion may in fact be an immovable force, while another who you thought would never convert in a million years finds her way back to the faith with ease. Often, it is those who seem closest who are the hardest to inch back in. They are comfortable where they are, just "being a good person," while those who are farther away make the trip more swiftly. No matter; there isn't a simple recipe for conversions, but there is an art to helping others move in that direction.

When still archbishop of Buenos Aires, before becoming Pope Francis, Cardinal Bergoglio set up a parish network to assist the poor. When Argentina was hit by an economic crash, his network helped many thousands of people who had lost everything manage basic needs. Those in need, the future pope made clear to his parish network, were not to be viewed as cogs in a machine, but treated as unique individuals with their dignity intact. He asked the aid workers to view their efforts as "artisanal and not industrial."[1] Evangelization needs to be approached in much the same way: not as a formulaic, one-size-fits all, but as an artisanal approach, tailored to the needs of those you love.

This book also came together with the release of Pope Francis's apostolic exhortation, *Evangelii Gaudium* (*The Joy of the Gospel*), wherein he offers a treasure trove of ideas and encouragement for living our faith as evangelists. In his work, the pope reminds us that conversions happen upon God's agenda:

> *[I]t would be wrong to see it as a heroic individual undertaking, for it is first and foremost the Lord's work, surpassing anything which we can see and understand. Jesus is 'the first and greatest evangelizer.'*[2]

"In every activity of evangelization," the pope explains, "the primacy always belongs to God, who has called us to cooperate with him and who leads us on by the power of his Spirit. The real newness is the newness which God himself mysteriously brings about and inspires, provokes, guides and accompanies in a thousand ways."[3]

And because the hard work of evangelization is the work of God and not a scientific theory, it is unpredictable. As a result, Pope Francis reminds us, "The Gospel speaks of a seed which, once sown, grows by itself, even as the farmer sleeps. The Church has to accept this unruly freedom of the word, which accomplishes what it wills in ways that surpass our calculations and ways of thinking."[4]

Writing of his own conversion, Austin Ruse, president of C-Fam (Center for Family & Human Rights), a pro-life lobby at the United Nations, says, "Any convert can look back upon his journey and see the tugs even if he didn't notice them at the time. Converts lovingly remember and talk about the times that God called out to them. They talk about that conversation, that time they laid upon the grass, the time they met a priest, that errant comment by a stupid professor. Each of these is God calling out to follow Him."[5]

Perhaps more important, we need to keep in mind that conversion often isn't just one move, but many different turns toward God. In many ways, we are all called to conversion: to draw ourselves closer to our Lord. It is an ongoing process, and part of the process is fulfilled by giving our own faith away to others. It is in this life-giving act that we find a sense of mission and great joy.

Pope Francis explains, "'Life grows by being given away, and it weakens in isolation and comfort. Indeed, those who enjoy life most are those who leave security on the shore and become excited by the mission of communicating life to others.' When the Church summons Christians to take up the task of evangelization, she is simply pointing to the source of authentic personal fulfillment."[6]

Evangelization isn't just about helping others, but about fulfilling our own mission as Catholics, which when fruitful is graced with the deepest desires of the human heart: joy and peace.

Our culture is currently plagued by a tyranny of niceness, where being pleasant is mistaken for authentic love. Religion and politics shouldn't be discussed in polite company, lest anyone be made uncomfortable. What Pope Benedict XVI called "the tyranny of relativism" has made it socially unnecessary to speak of religion, as one faith is just as good as the next, or so the culture dictates. These pressures make the effort at evangelization particularly difficult because of the premium placed on niceness and not ruffling feathers. Going out of our comfort zone to win converts can be overwhelming, but there is no reason to reinvent the wheel every time.

When listening to converts, we hear some common patterns among their conversion stories. "It was the kindness of a stranger who showed me mercy." "It was reading a book that someone loaned me at just the right time in my life." Sometimes it is a lot of little things, which finally culminate in a transformed life. It is these patterns that will be looked at carefully in this book.

The first chapter looks at the importance of living our own faith, and how conversions are the fruit of a mature faith. It is a basic tenet of economics that you can't give what you don't have. This holds true in spiritual economy. If you don't have faith, you don't live it; if you don't pray, your efforts will fall short. Additionally, this chapter will look at how evangelization and a deep desire to spread our faith are a necessary part of living our faith.

Prayer is, of course, a no-brainer when it comes to evangelization, but it is the essential place to start. As we will see in chapter one, it is clear we are cooperating with God to convert hearts, so chapter two looks at prayer as the conduit through which we can come to know and understand his will. The chapter will look at several types of prayers and novenas and their applicability to evangelization.

There are some basic tools required for any project, and evangelization is no exception. Chapter three pulls together a list of tools, such as charity, hospitality, and humor, that can be called upon in the actual work of sharing Christ's message with others.

The phrase "offer it up" is used so often, many people dismiss it out of hand. But just because it seems trite doesn't mean it lacks real effectiveness. The saints over the centuries have made it clear that suffering, when united with Christ's, is pure spiritual gold. Chapter four delves into the mystery of suffering and its fruits, seen and unseen.

The Gospels are full of examples of Christ asking questions, because asking questions has the disarming effect of making people think about a topic in a new light. Chapter five explores the art of asking questions, as well as knowing when to speak and when to keep quiet.

Unfortunately, far too many Catholics have been poorly catechized and substantial misconceptions about our faith abound among non-Catholics. Chapter six discusses the vital importance of being prepared to help those with questions about the faith. You don't have to possess a wealth of knowledge, but you do need to know where to find the right resources to pass along.

A wise priest once told me that culture is "God's love made visible." As evidenced by the popularity of movies such as *The Passion of The Christ*, the world is starving for more than cheap entertainment. But do we really seek it and help promote it in our lives? Chapter seven considers the importance of promoting authentic culture and how beauty, even in small ways, points others back the Maker of the true, the good, and the beautiful.

Finally, many of us face the very difficult reality that those we love are either approaching death or have died without the benefit of the sacraments. Chapter eight looks at the light of hope, especially in the great darkness of the most tragic of cases, in which all seems lost, such as suicide or a sudden death. The Church throughout the centuries has made it clear that God's mercy is enduring, particularly through the promise of purgatory.

Our Lady plays a special role in conversions. After the Spanish arrived in the Americas, every effort was made at converting the natives. Only after Our Lady of Guadalupe made her appearances to Juan Diego did the floodgates of evangelization open up in Mexico and beyond. Every effort at conversion should rely upon Mary's intercession.

So before moving on to the main content of this book, we start, like we start all good things, with prayer. We pray with Pope Francis:

> *We implore [Mary's] maternal intercession that the Church may become a home for many peoples, a mother for all peoples, and that the way may be opened to the birth of a new world. It is the Risen Christ who tells us, with a power that fills us with confidence and unshakable hope: "Behold, I make all things new." (Revelation 21:5)*[7]

One

LIVING WITNESS: CONVERTS ARE THE FRUIT OF A MATURE FAITH

Outspoken atheist and comedian Penn Jillette—really the last person you'd expect would have something good to say about religion—recently made a very startling statement:

> *If you believe that there's a heaven and a hell, and people could be going to hell or not getting eternal life, and you think that it's not really worth telling them this because it would make it socially awkward . . . how much do you have to hate somebody to not proselytize? How much do you have to hate somebody to believe everlasting life is possible and not tell them that?*
>
> *I mean, if I believed, beyond the shadow of a doubt, that a truck was coming at you, and you didn't believe that truck was bearing down on you, there is a certain point where I tackle you. And this is more important than that.*[1]

This is a strong statement, particularly from an atheist. While I'm not sure how many people have had success tackling someone into the faith (and no, please don't try this at home), there are clearly other ways to respond to God's call. Jillette's point does underline, however, both the urgency of our time here on earth and the gravity of the situation. We want people to convert not for superficial reasons, but because it truly is a matter of eternal life and death. Even a cursory glance as testimonies of the saints about hell, like St. Teresa of Avila who was shown the place the devil had prepared for her because of her sins, are enough to motivate anyone to roll up their sleeves.[2] As confirmed Catholics, it is, in fact, our duty and our responsibility to pass on the faith to others.

A lot has been written about evangelization, but the one element Pope Francis makes clear is that evangelization is the fruit of a mature faith. You simply cannot give what you don't have. And while it may seem that if you just said the right thing to your teenage son or could get your neighbor to read the right book, they would convert, these simple things, while they could have some effect, most likely will not be enough to truly bring them a deep and abiding faith. No quick tips, tricks, or gospel tracts will do. Just wishing and hoping that your grown daughter will return to the Church will not make it happen. If you desire to make converts, you first must convert yourself.

As Pope Francis explains:

> *This is why we evangelize. A true missionary, who never ceases to be a disciple, knows that Jesus walks with him, speaks to him, breathes with him, works with him. He senses Jesus alive with him in the midst of the missionary enterprise. Unless we see him present at the heart of our missionary commitment, our enthusiasm soon wanes and we are no longer sure of what it is that we are handing on; we lack vigor and passion. A person who*

> *is not convinced, enthusiastic, certain and in love, will convince nobody.*[3]

Fr. Dwight Longenecker, a convert, priest, and blogger, has written about how most Catholics don't live with the expectation that their faith can "do" anything for them. "They have been taught to fulfill their duties and say their prayers, and they give at least lip service to the beliefs that confession really absolves them of their sins. . . . But they don't expect the daily surge of God's power in their lives."[4]

How, then, can someone who is lukewarm about his faith live with any expectation that others should live with it as well? Living the life of a lukewarm Catholic has no attraction because their hearts are not open to God really doing something in their lives.

Moreover, Pope Francis warns us that "[t]hose who speak as Christians, but do not act as Christians, do harm to the faith." Christians, the pope explains, need to examine their words and actions to ensure that they are sincere, especially speaking about the faith: "[A] Christian word without Christ at its center leads to vanity, to pride, power for the sake of power."[5]

"If we do not feel an intense desire to share this love," the Holy Father explains, "we need to pray insistently that he will once more touch our hearts. We need to implore his grace daily, asking him to open our cold hearts and shake up our lukewarm and superficial existence."[6]

So, if you are not attending Mass and going to confession regularly, you should consider putting this book down for several months, get your sacramental life back in order, and then pick it up again. This book is full of tools, and all tools, even spiritual tools, can be dangerous if not used properly. If you aren't living the faith, how can you expect others to?

We all know how hard it is to change ourselves, but it is much easier to change ourselves than another person. And sometimes the changes we make in ourselves can be the spark of grace to help others change.

Can the Blind Lead the Blind?

In Luke's Gospel, Jesus asks the very simple question, "Can a blind person guide a blind person? Will not both fall into a pit?" (Luke 6:39) While chapter six will discuss the important role of education in evangelization, what I believe Christ is getting at here is more to the heart of the issue: the *why* behind a conversion.

I've seen many relationships in which the husband converts for the wife, or vice versa, but the hearts of both are still cold. While some of these cases have come to good effect, more often than not they don't. Why? Because you can't give what you don't have. If you don't love God, love the Church, or know Christ, it is going to be very difficult to inspire that in another.

Take, for example, one couple I know, Seamus and Abigail. Seamus had a tepid faith, leaning mostly upon his family's traditions and habits. His fiancée joined the Church to please him and his family. But what happened was that Abigail not only was better catechized than Seamus, she also began to really believe in what the Church taught. She joined other women once a week in a prayer group led by a priest, during which they engaged in rich conversation in addition to prayer. Over time Seamus became resentful of Abigail's faith and her conviction about the Church's teachings, especially on premarital sex. It didn't take long for the tension in their relationship to become too much for Abigail to continue to fight. Ironically, she had to choose between the Church and him. Without a strong enough foundation or the tools to pass along her own faith to her fiancé, Abigail abandoned her living faith for Seamus's comfortable corner of cafeteria Catholicism.

Living in Community

There once was an old woman who stopped going to church. She decided it wasn't really doing anything for her, so making the effort was no longer necessary. She would just pray at home. Her parish priest noticed her absence. Concerned that perhaps something was wrong, he went to her home to check on her. She let him in, assured him all was fine, but explained that she no longer needed to go to Mass. Sitting down in front of a fire, the priest fell silent and the two sat and watched the flames lick the sides of the fireplace for some time.

After a long silence, once the flames were reduced to embers, the priest went over to the fire and took out one large, red burning coal. He set it out on the hearth and sat back in his chair in silence. As the two watched, the embers in the fire continued to glow red and orange, while the solitary ember on the hearth quickly lost all of its color and was reduced to a clump of black ash. Soon thereafter the priest left. And a few days later he saw the old woman once again in the pews. His silent message had been clear: The Church is the fuel of our faith. Without it, the heat and zeal of faith can only burn so long.

Statistically, because fewer people are getting married and staying married, more and more people live outside anything resembling a community (and no, dogs don't count). This reality of isolation is a source of great loneliness and unhappiness. So many opportunities to love and receive love from those God has put into our lives are missed.

Pope John Paul II wrote extensively, particularly in *The Theology of the Body*, about the sincere gift of self, and how only when we give ourselves away do we truly find ourselves. It is a profound mystery, one of those secrets hidden in plain sight for those with the eyes to see.

Pope Francis reminds us of the importance of engaging in relationships and serving those beyond our own tight and small circle of friends and family. Frequently, he explains, "believers seek to hide or keep apart from others, or quietly flit from one place to another or from one task to another, without creating deep and stable bonds."[7] Without such bonds, we can never find an authentic source of self-giving. We will likely find plenty of "me time" and be surrounded by a lot of stuff, but a deep and abiding happiness will be missing.

Looking at history, healthy cultures understood this essential key not only to personal happiness, but for flourishing as a community (even if it wasn't always acted upon or openly articulated). The gift of self, or on a broader scale, "our lives for theirs," has animated history for centuries. Think of the building of Notre Dame Cathedral in Paris, which the early masons knew would never be finished in their lifetimes. It can be lived out within a family, a parish, a city, and a country. It is when a culture ceases to see the value in the gift of self for others—when it decides "their lives for mine," like we currently see in abortion and embryonic stem cell research, for example—that a society will approach rapid decline.

Evangelization Is Essential

Evangelization is part of the idea of "my life for yours" and the gift of self. Someone wise once said, "Evangelization is one beggar telling another where to find bread." At the heart of it, we are all beggars. We need other human beings for our survival, while we are also radically dependent upon God for our existence. All of us can point to someone who has passed along the faith to us, through word and deed or simply by example. Our faith is not meant to be kept under a bushel; it's meant to be shared. It is essential not only for others, but for our own continued spiritual growth. If we do not share what we have been given, then the gift was never truly received. Every gift given is meant to be passed along.

As the pope explains:

> *When the Church summons Christians to take up the task of evangelization, she is simply pointing to the source of authentic personal fulfillment. For "here we discover a profound law of reality: that life is attained and matures in the measure that it is offered up in order to give life to others."*[8]

Pope Francis challenges us to also see evangelization as an essential part of our own spiritual growth. The benefits are not just for the other person, but like so many gifts of the faith, have a reciprocal effect when we act in relationship with someone else. Their good is also our good, which can be difficult to discern when we live by the mantra of "What's in it for me?"

"Every authentic experience of truth and goodness seeks by its very nature to grow within us, and any person who has experienced a profound liberation becomes more sensitive to the needs of others," the pope explains, adding, "As it expands, goodness takes root and develops. If we wish to lead a dignified and fulfilling life, we have to reach out to others and seek their good."[9]

Living with Joy and Peace

So many of us think, "I would be a much better Catholic if I didn't have to deal with X. X is a real stumbling block for me." Saints, however, are not made because they didn't have to deal with a lousy boss, or a particular illness, or whatever your cross may be; they are saints because they *did* deal with these things, and frequently much more. Sts. Anthony of the

Desert and Padre Pio frequently spent the night fighting demons, who would bloody them to a pulp. Being a true witness doesn't mean living with the absence of conflict or turmoil; it means facing all of it with the virtues of Christ, particularly a joyful and peaceful heart.

The pope encourages us to be joyful witnesses:

> *[A]n evangelizer must never look like someone who has just come back from a funeral! Let us recover and deepen our enthusiasm, that "delightful and comforting joy of evangelizing, even when it is in tears that we must sow. And may the world of our time, which is searching, sometimes with anguish, sometimes with hope, be enabled to receive the good news not from evangelizers who are dejected, discouraged, impatient or anxious, but from ministers of the Gospel whose lives glow with fervour, who have first received the joy of Christ.*[10]

Sometimes living joyfully or as a faithful witness is the hardest of all. It is difficult to remember that our actions speak so much louder than our words. And even more so if our actions are angry, gruff, proud, boastful, mean, or sad. Yes, the world is a heavy place, but we can't be all cross and no resurrection. St. Teresa of Ávila used to say, "May God protect me from dour saints." After all, there is nothing more attractive than the face of joyful holiness, for, as Pope Francis wrote at the start of *Evangelii Gaudium*, "The joy of the gospel fills the hearts and lives of all who encounter Jesus."[11]

For those people who just can't do joy, whose temperament simply isn't going to be joyful, there is another clear hallmark of holiness that can be a strong witness: peacefulness. For a long time, I thought about these words of Christ during the Mass: "My peace I give to you; my peace I leave with you." (John 14:27) Christ is very clear on this. He has *already* given us his peace. It is there for the taking. Our charge is simply to use it. He has left it, so it isn't going anywhere.

Our world is characterized by chaos, when simply reading the news can give you emotional whiplash. So an individual or a family remaining calm and peaceful in the midst of great turmoil speaks volumes.

Do All Things in Christ

A wise priest I know once asked God in prayer why the evangelization of the world happened mainly in the Western Hemisphere, with very little foothold in Asia. In his heart the aged priest heard the Lord tell him that people stopped evangelizing *in* Christ. They did things *for* Christ and *with* Christ, but not *in* him.

Every Sunday at Mass and every daily Mass, these words are heard during the Consecration: "Through him, with him, in him, in the unity of the Holy Spirit, all glory and honor is yours, Almighty Father, forever and ever. Amen." Let these words be a reminder to us today and always as we try to renew hearts *in* Christ.

Two

PRAYER: RECEIVING GOD'S MESSAGE

As Pope Francis has made clear, God is at the helm of the conversion process. Our role (and privilege) is to assist God in bringing others to the faith. The only way to do this, though, is through a steady diet of prayer. Prayer is the means of communication though which we find out the directives God wants to give us to assist others. When we are praying regularly, our discernment goes from trying to interpret the hand gestures of a first base coach when we are not on the team to having that coach whisper directly into our ears exactly what we should do. It is an absolute essential.

When I was in graduate school, my spiritual director wisely insisted that I spend an hour in daily prayer at Adoration. I thought he was nuts. How was I ever going to do that with a full load of classes, a full-time job, and daily Mass? As a single woman, without a husband or family to look after, I obediently followed his advice. I knew my life wouldn't always be so flexible and that it would be a great opportunity to pray for the conversions of my immediate family—my mother and siblings, as well as my late father, not knowing if he was in purgatory or heaven. Nightly I would trudge to the adoration chapel. There, for an hour every evening, I would kneel in prayer for my loved ones. And of course, it changed my life. I had a new clarity about things that had seemed muddled before, and I had a deep and abiding peace. When the peace was shaken, I knew I had an appointment with our Lord to help me comb out whatever knots had arisen in the day. And I started to see real fruit in the lives of my family. Since that time my mother and every one of my siblings have reverted to the faith.

We are not alone in securing our sanctification. Each one of us has had someone somewhere praying for us, offering sacrifices, even if they were unaware of whom they were assisting. There is a beautiful medieval statement that says, "*Bonum est diffusivum sui*," or "The good pours itself out." The good that we do does not just stay with us, but is mysteriously connected to those around us. This can be seen easily among families, when the parents are continually giving everything they have to protect their marriage and raise their children. We can also see it materially through tithing and through gifts made to help those in need. Less easy to see are the spiritual works, many of which happen unbeknownst to us in heaven or in purgatory, that have resplendent effects in our own lives.

It is also easy to see how the bad pours itself out—we can observe the effects the sins of others have upon our own lives, especially in the form of drugs or violence. Even the so-called victimless sins are really not victimless, but can have rippling negative effects, although they may be more difficult to see. Often those sorts of sin are sins of omission, things someone ought to have done but didn't. The movies *It's a Wonderful Life* and *A Christmas Carol* are great reminders of these realities.

Because the good that we do spills over into the lives others, prayer is one of those goods that help both the one praying and those who are being prayed for. As our relationship with the Trinity grows, the fruits of this relationship also spread to those around us. As such, Pope Francis reminds us of the distance prayer can go:

> *How good it is to stand before a crucifix, or on our knees before the Blessed Sacrament, and simply to be in his presence! How much good it does us when he once more touches our lives and impels us to share his new life! What then happens is that "we speak of what we have seen and heard" (1 Jn 1:3). The best incentive for sharing the Gospel comes from contemplating it with love, lingering over its pages and reading it with the heart. If we approach it in this way, its beauty will amaze and constantly excite us.*[1]

This cannot happen automatically, Francis warns. "But if this is to come about, we need to recover a contemplative spirit which can help us to realize ever anew that we have been entrusted with a treasure which makes us more human and helps us to lead a new life. There is nothing more precious which we can give to others."[2] Indeed, the good we do does not remain just with us.

Prayer can come in many different forms: Mass, Adoration, the Rosary, praise and gratitude, intercessory prayer, praying with others, and Lectio Divina. All of these have a different role to play when we're helping others find their spiritual home in the Church. When these types of prayer are engaged in on a regular basis, our souls can become more nimble in responding to God's requests and his will. God, who is the font of all goodness, diffuses his goodness to us and then through us.

Mass

The saints have made it clear that it is not possible to overstate the importance of the Mass. It is "the source and summit of Christian Life";[3] there is nothing more important that we can do than to go each day to attend the unbloody sacrifice of Christ's crucifixion. Catherine Doherty, the foundress of the Madonna House Apostolate, whose cause is up for canonization, speaks of what happens when we attend Mass, particularly daily Mass:

> *Our horizons become wider than all the universe, for they span time and eternity. Love grows within our soul until finally its eyes see Christ in all. Slowly, but oh, how surely, our whole person turns to God! Then the spirit of . . . poverty, chastity, and obedience, of the Beatitudes and the Ten Commandments becomes simple and clear. We become free. How free cannot be told; it has to be experienced.*[4]

What Doherty describes makes perfect sense in the spirit of the prayer of St. John the Baptist: "He must increase; I must decrease" (John 3:30). Christ, in the Eucharist, is transforming our souls to look more like his, and therefore to experience more of who he is.

While there are many things that happen at Mass, as the Church's most powerful prayer, the Eucharist is where our petitions for others can be most quickly answered when united with Christ's offering. There are many different novenas and promises associated with the Mass, such as the booklet *The Two Divine Promises*.

There are, of course, seasons of our lives when getting to Mass is easier than others. When attending daily Mass is not an option, we can always unite ourselves to Christ through a prayer of spiritual communion, inviting him into our hearts.

Adoration

Adoration is the place where we can meet Christ face-to-face, but without words. Often people bring a book to read while in Adoration, but that is a bit odd. A nun who was very practiced in the art of contemplation once said, "Would you ever meet a friend for lunch, but instead of talking directly to him, sit and read a letter he had written to you?" That is what it is like when we are not directly engaging Christ in front of us. It is through this silence that any and every issue can be addressed—or none at all. Just looking at him, gazing upon the Savior of the world, should be enough to fill us with wonder.

The only experience I have had that compares at all to the wonder at Adoration was after my first child was born. I could just sit and look at her for hours—tiny fingers, toes lined up in a perfect row, sweet coos, and her peaceful sleep; I just sat in awe of how this little person came into the world *through me*. Of course, contemplation of Christ is a much higher reality and, naturally, we don't worship our children, but there was a similarity I have not been able to compare with anything else.

While the fruit of Adoration may not be immediately apparent, over time it reveals itself more through what you say to others and how you say it, particularly as your own heart continues to be transformed.

The Rosary

The Rosary is also an essential prayer, particularly for the needs of others. My friend Nicole met the most wonderful man in college. The problem was that he was Protestant, and his mother was a senior administrator at a Protestant college. For James to convert would cause serious pain and discord to his entire family. Nicole, however, feeling deeply that James was the man she was to marry, went to the Rosary. She started praying a fifty-four-day novena—twenty-seven days of petition and twenty-seven days of thanksgiving—a mystery of the Rosary each day. By the end of the fifty-four days, James was ready to become a Catholic, despite his mother's objections.

The Rosary also provides us with a way of contemplating Christ's life, through the twenty decades, broken up into four mysteries, chronicling his ministry. Knowing the life of Christ and his mother always makes it easier to imitate them.

Prayers of Praise and Gratitude

Catholic speaker Matthew Kelly often says, "Joy is the fruit of appreciation." Appreciation can become a font from which we can truly live out a joyful witness for others, particularly if joy doesn't come easily to us.

We can first live with a spirit of gratefulness for all that God has bestowed upon us, but also in gratitude for the people in our lives, no matter what their circumstances. As our pope points out, "Far from being suspicious, negative and despairing, it is a spiritual gaze born of deep faith which acknowledges what God is doing in the lives of others. At the same time, it is the gratitude which flows from a heart attentive to others."[5]

Gratitude, according to the pope, can be grease in the wheels of those who labor in the harvest. "When evangelizers rise from prayer, their hearts are more open; freed of self-absorption, they are desirous of doing good and sharing their lives with others."[6]

When I first moved to Rome, my friend Anne joined me for Christmas. A convert, Anne had spent years trying to learn to praise God in every circumstance, even when terrible things happened, knowing that it was his holy will that allowed them. Walking home to my apartment one evening, we passed the Colosseum. On the street side, Anne let down her guard and carried her large purse by the handles, unwittingly dangling it near the passing traffic. And sure enough, someone drove by and swiped it out of her hand. Of course we ran after the car, but it was hopeless. As she panted to catch her breath, Anne said over and over again, "Praise God. Praise God." She later told me that she had been mugged three times in her life—once in Washington, D.C., another time on the Metro in

Paris, and then this time in Rome. She was so grateful that she had finally gotten the response right. Instead of anger and fear, she was able to praise God, even in a frightening and difficult situation.

We too can praise God even when our best efforts seem to be bearing no fruit, transforming even the worst of situations into hope instead of despair.

Intercessory Prayer

Intercession is an integral part of evangelical work. Planted in the soil of Mass, Adoration, the Rosary, and deep gratitude, prayers for others are deeply effective. As the pope explains, "The great men and women of God were great intercessors."[7] This is not to say that intercessory prayer is something added on top of contemplation and other types of prayer. The pope assures us that "intercessory prayer does not divert us from true contemplation, since authentic contemplation always has a place for others."[8] As St. Paul says, "I constantly pray with you in every one of my prayers for all of you...because I hold you in my heart" (Philippians 1:4, 7).

Comparing intercession to a leaven, such as yeast, the pope explains how it expands in the heart of the Trinity.

> *It is a way of penetrating the Father's heart and discovering new dimensions which can shed light on concrete situations and change them. We can say that God's heart is touched by our intercession, yet in reality he is always there first. What our intercession achieves is that his power, his love and his faithfulness are shown ever more clearly in the midst of the people.*[9]

The pope is showing us that the way to truly meet the needs of others is through intercessory prayer couched in other types of daily prayer.

In my own family, when it was clear that my efforts to guide my sister to the faith weren't working, I prayed that someone else would come into her life to "seal the deal." Shortly thereafter, on a business trip, my sister restlessly went to three restaurants to find dinner. At the third place—though she hates smoke and rarely sits at bars—she sat down at the bar next to an older woman who was smoking.

She and the smoker, Veronica—a devout Catholic—started chatting, and before the meal was over, they were fast friends. Veronica and her husband were instrumental in bringing my sister back to the Church. They even took her to Rome for a private audience with Pope John Paul II. My sister, now a homeschooling mother of seven, still marvels at meeting Veronica and the impact one person can have on a life.

Sometimes we encounter situations in which our own gifts are inadequate to meet the needs of a particular individual. What that person needs is simply beyond what we can do. But it is not beyond what Christ can do. Particularly in our decadent and broken culture, there are few who have not been touched in one way or another by contraception, abortion, the occult, substance abuse, or sexual abuse. So many people bear the scars and open wounds from these spiritual—and sometimes material and emotional—diseases. It is also important to be mindful of this reality and, particularly if you know of such a history in someone's life, to pray hard for healing to Christ the Healer.

There will be occasions when we may know what might help someone, but because of brokenness, distance, or sin, we may only be able to pray for them. I encountered this recently with another mother at my daughter's school. Despite common friends and experiences, our personalities are like oil and water. Conceding that I would never be able to reach this mother through word or example, I realized the only real option left was prayer. So I pray a Hail Mary for her every time we see each other in the drop-off line at school. I pray for her when I see her driving around town. I pray for her when I see her name on a sign-up list for school-related activities. I don't ever anticipate our relationship changing, but my prayer does two things: It keeps my mind and heart focused on what I can truly do to love her, and it inoculates me from the painful emotions I might feel if I let her disdain get to me. Being snubbed by others is never a pleasant experience, but it is one we will face if we are truly following the gospel. It is a relief to have found a way to maneuver through it instead of letting its weight discourage me.

Unfortunately there are scores of people out there who have, in one way or another, been hurt by Catholics—whether is be laity, religious, or priests. Often the deep and painful wounds result in anger directed at the entire Church. In these cases too, prayer and fasting to Christ the Healer may be the only route to help.

Lectio Divina

As Pope Francis has made clear, the best way to find zeal for the Gospels is to spend time poring over them, reading and rereading them, and contemplating them deeply in our hearts. St. Jerome said, "Ignorance of Scripture means ignorance of Christ." As we become more and more familiar with the life of Christ and the fingerprints of God in both the Old and New Testaments, it becomes easier to share his Word, his heart, and his message with others. Lectio Divina, or divine reading, is the ancient four-part practice of reading a passage from Scripture, meditating on it, praying, and then contemplating Our Lord. It is meant as a tool to draw us closer to God using Scripture as a living word from him instead of merely as an ancient document to be studied. Lectio Divina provides another avenue to hear God's call directly through the Bible, and to grow in understanding the mind of Christ in order to act more like Christ.

Praying with Others

As Christ promised, "For where two or three are gathered together in my name, there am I in the midst of them" (Matthew 18:20). Praying with others can be enormously fruitful in the conversion of hearts. In college, I started praying the Rosary once a week with a group of wonderful women. In addition to the experience of praying regularly with other women of faith, through them I learned much about Catholicism as they shared their knowledge. Often, after we prayed, we would go get coffee. Because of the nature of our time together, our conversations were edifying and didn't devolve into gossip or other superficialities, making it a joy to spend time with these women. Having a scheduled time to pray with others also kept me more accountable for regularly praying the Rosary.

It is always a consolation to know that others are praying with you for an intention. It is the life, mission, and duty of cloistered nuns and monks to pray for the salvation of souls through prayer, suffering, and sacrifices. They welcome prayer requests and usually have a way of receiving them either by phone or the Internet. By contacting a local order, or elsewhere around the world, one is assured that the professionals close to the heart of God are offering up one's intentions.

Praying Always

Jesus invites us to pray always (see Luke 18:1). Ultimately prayer is a very flexible tool and gift, particularly suited to trying to meet the needs of everyone in our lives, either through the types we've discussed or through a more simple act of uniting ourselves with God. Through it, God also gives us insights about how to address a situation, when to ask for help, and when we need to back off from something altogether because a situation is beyond our limits. It can be summed up well in the simple Serenity Prayer:

> *God, grant me the serenity to accept the things I cannot change, the courage to change the things I can, and wisdom to know the difference.*

Three

THE BASICS

After I came to understand what a treasure I had in the Church, I *really* wanted my family members to find that same love. Unfortunately my family viewed my conversion as either a "nice new hobby" or, more sinisterly, as cultish behavior. I recall my mother having my very heterodox Catholic godfather call me to talk me out of being so, well, Catholic. While I can't recall the particulars of the conversation, it sure didn't have the intended effect. I had lived a watered-down version of Catholicism for decades and rejected its emptiness.

My efforts to convert my family weren't always the most graceful or grace-filled. I made the rookie errors most zealous converts do and was too pushy, too eager to tell them everything I knew, or was simply misinformed about Church teaching. After months of seeing my best-laid arguments gain no ground, I turned to prayer.

It was in prayer that I realized that God loved all of these people more than I did. And he wanted them to come home to the Catholic faith more than I did. I rested in that for a while, and finally it became my plea. "God, you love them more than I do," I would say over and over again, which I found freed me up from working so ineffectively. I let them be who they were and just loved them right where they were instead of as I hoped they would be.

Little by little, big changes started to happen. I found our relationships to be more joyful as I focused on them and what could make them happy instead of how I would make them happy by telling them to be faithful Catholics.

The human heart responds to pressure. Think of a slick piece of ice on a smooth tabletop. The more pressure placed upon it, the farther and more swiftly it slides away. But gentle pressure keeps the ice in place. Conversions are like this. The more we want a loved one to convert on our time and our terms, the more it eludes us. Remove the pressure and the conversion is much more likely to happen. Impatience, hostility, and other superficial motivations are the kind of pressure that the human heart cannot bear. Instead, the heart responds to the gentle pressures of joy, kindness, mercy, and patience.

After looking at hundreds of conversion stories, I found that certain patterns began to emerge among those doing the converting. Most projects involve a set of tools, supplies, or ingredients necessary before the actual work can be started. The following elements comprise that list of things that can make the heavy lifting of converting hearts much lighter. While we may not be called to use all of them, it is good to know what is available to help bring Christ's light and love to others.

Charity: Love People Where They Are

We all have a sense when people are trying to get us to do something that seems more about them than about us. Sharing our faith is no different if we put our agenda ahead of showing real, other-centered love. It is important for others to know that we love them for them, not just because we hope they will share the same love for Christ. While that is a wonderful blessing to share among friends and family, it is not the only basis we have for loving others.

A mistake often made in evangelization is to allow the actions of their away-from-the-Church friends/children/spouse, etc., to bring them to great despair, impatience, and exasperation, all of which colors their relationship. And it is easy to see that we can sometimes withhold our love and affection from others, even children, "until they become Catholic." Such an attitude frustrates even the best-intentioned effort. This is not to say that we have to embrace every aspect of their lives, especially those elements that are sinful, but we need to really come to know who they are—their gifts, interests, and goals. In knowing these it is easier to make suggestions or draw out conversations related to our faith in a way that could be helpful, not cold or pushy. Authentic love, as we have all heard in 1 Corinthians 13, is kind and patient, enduring all things for the beloved. Such love, one convert has said, "is the bridge over which truth can flow."[1]

As Pope Francis explains in *Evangelii Gaudium*:

> *Jesus himself is the model of this method of evangelization which brings us to the very heart of his people. How good it is for us to contemplate the closeness which he shows to everyone! If he speaks to someone, he looks into their eyes with deep love and concern: "Jesus, looking upon him, loved him" (Mk 10:21). We see how accessible he is, as he draws near the blind man and eats and drinks with sinners without worrying about being thought a glutton and a drunkard himself. We see his sensitivity in allowing a sinful woman to anoint his feet and in receiving Nicodemus by night.*[2]

Here Jesus is embracing people where they are, but not embracing their sins. It is his love that calls them to something better.

This effort, Pope Francis makes clear, is not meant to be heavy or dour work. Our efforts are not seen to be merely of "a sense of obligation, not as a burdensome duty, but as the result of a personal decision which brings us joy and gives meaning to our lives."[3]

So often joy is missing from these difficult relationships among loved ones. Guilt, anger, and sorrow usually prevail, but what the pope is describing is really a sense of mission, of following Christ's model to love the beloved, warts and all, no matter the cost or consequences.

Pope Francis points to what he calls a Marian style of Catholic evangelization. "Whenever we look to Mary, we come to believe once again in the revolutionary nature of love and tenderness. In her we see that humility and tenderness are not virtues of the weak but of the strong who need not treat others poorly in order to feel important themselves."[4] This Marian style is marked by the "interplay of justice and tenderness, of contemplation and concern for others."[5]

Say and Do Something

Shortly after my reversion to the faith, I heard the words often attributed to St. Francis: "Preach always. Use words only when necessary." It was as if a great burden had been taken off my back. I didn't need to always find the right thing to say or do around those who had fallen away from the faith. I just needed to live the faith the best way that I knew how.

While I still agree that this is great advice, I think it falls short in many ways, especially for those of us who get comfortable doing nothing, or being passive, or who simply don't want to rock the boat. St. Francis said, "Use words only when necessary." Sometimes words *are* necessary. You can't bear fruit if you aren't willing to sow the seeds.

Most converts point to something specific—an event or a series of events—that happened in their life leading them to Christ. While being around people who are truly living the faith with joy is a great boost, more is usually required.

Many popular spiritual practices want to avoid reaching out to others. Pope Francis points out that "we see the growing attraction to various forms of a 'spirituality of well-being' divorced from any community life, or to a 'theology of prosperity' detached from responsibility for our brothers and sisters, or to depersonalized experiences which are nothing more than a form of self-centredness."[6] Focusing upon only our own needs flies in the face of the gospel message without the leaven of true works.

"Many try to escape from others and take refuge in the comfort of their privacy or in a small circle of close friends, renouncing the realism of the social aspect of the Gospel," states the Holy Father. "Meanwhile," he adds, "the Gospel tells us constantly to run the risk of a face-to-face encounter with others, with their physical presence which challenges us, with their pain and their pleas, with their joy which infects us in our close and continuous interaction."[7]

Author Joseph Pearce, in his book *Race with the Devil: My Journey from Racial Hatred to Rational Love*, speaks of specific acts of mercy performed by perfect strangers as the source of his own conversion. Pearce confesses that in two of the cases, he was either drunk or lying when the strangers offered him mercy that he did not deserve. It seems to be a truism that those who need the most love can be the hardest to love. But the fact that it is difficult to love someone doesn't mean that we shouldn't do it. As Pearce has made clear, it was precisely because he was shown the love of mercy when he didn't deserve it that his heart was changed.

Rather than see us keep difficult people at arm's length, Pope Francis reminds us, "Jesus wants us to touch human misery, to touch the suffering flesh of others. He hopes that we will stop looking for those personal or communal niches which shelter us from the maelstrom of human misfortune and instead enter into the reality of other people's lives and know the power of tenderness." Not only does this tenderness and mercy transform them, it brings fruit to our lives. "Whenever we do so, our lives become wonderfully complicated and we experience intensely what it is to be a people, to be part of a people."[8]

Act with Your Particular Audience in Mind

One of the most important steps we can take is to come to know our audience. A good example of *not* knowing your audience involves me trying to convert a friend. Pulling out my shiny new arguments for God's existence, I thought, "Surely, these will be convincing." Right. In retrospect, although embarrassing, this memory makes me smile because my poor friend Erin was not the type of girl to be won over by anything remotely intellectual. Not that she wasn't bright, it just wasn't something that meant much of anything to her. My proofs thudded to the floor like lead balloons.

Knowledge of your audience is key. Is your friend a reader? An intellectual? More of an emotional type? A movie buff? Sportsman? A foodie? The differing interests of a soul will give you important clues about what might be effective to reach his or her heart. Where we spend our time usually is where our heart is. Finding a medium that can reach that point of interest is a good step in the right direction. Apologetics come in various packages. Knowing a person's weaknesses or wounds could also prove to be insightful. Does he or she need logical arguments? Mercy? A good book? A combination? Nothing seems to work? Just prayer? Fasting or other sacrifices?

One convert, several years after her conversion, referred to all the prayers, bits of information, insights, and books that people passed along to her as "gifts from God." But these gifts need to be offered at the right time. Very often, if someone is not ready for what we are offering, it may be received like a large check given to a small child. It may be a wonderful gift, but the child doesn't yet have the maturity to understand exactly what has been given.

Sometimes, however, a conversion can take place with something completely beyond what you might expect to move a person. A proper Englishman, Mark, who used to break out in hives at the mere mention of religion, was asked by his wife to watch a video about a mystic who had experiences of the Virgin Mary. After reluctantly turning on the video, Mark was never the same. He sold the expensive car. He opened his heart to having more than two children. And he threw out his beloved movie collection. I'm not sure which of these was the most painful, but it has borne great fruit now that he is a Rite of Christian Initiation of Adults instructor and a proud father of a half-dozen redheads.

Prayer and discernment are important tools here. The Holy Spirit can inspire you to suggest something surprising but effective. We need to remain ever open to his promptings, without being attached to where the ideas lead. Only God knows.

Don't Overlook the Power of Hospitality

I recall spending the night as a child, along with my three siblings, at the home of two nuns next to our Catholic grade school. We prayed the Rosary in the chapel before bedtime and then stayed up late into the night talking about miracles and the saints. The night was full of peace, joy, and wonder. It was a long time before I experienced those feelings together again, but through the hospitality of good friends, I did. Previously I would have been hard-pressed to explain what was different about my time with those two nuns, or later in the homes of my Catholic friends, but I think David Clayton and Leila Marie Lawler, in their book, *The Little Oratory: A Beginner's Guide to Praying in the Home*, say it best:

> *The spirit of that home—that particular, unique home—is palpable to the visitor, just as the visitor feels something real upon entering a church. The stranger goes away taking a piece of it in his heart, being affirmed in his own unique calling. A person doesn't lose his identity upon being welcomed into a real, loving home; rather, he finds something in himself he didn't know before. The experience of being in a happy home draws forth love in its inhabitants and in its guests.*[9]

There is something very affirming about being welcomed into the home of praying Catholics, which had never occurred to me before, though I have experienced it over and over again. Passed along almost unwittingly, a home ordered in Christ speaks volumes about life lived in community. Even in large families, where one expects chaos, there is a happy rhythm. People are not moving from room to room, focused on one TV to the next, but are actually engaging each other, talking, storytelling, laughing, listening. Most guests will leave feeling loved, while those who lack faith will find the tug of something missing in their lives pulling a bit stronger than before.

In addition to prayer, numerous resources can be used to sanctify our homes, particularly when hosting others, such as holy water and blessed salt. Many people use them for blessing family members or sprinkling into cooking or beds, particularly in guest rooms, for a peaceful and protected night's sleep. Beautiful religious art, icons or statues, and relics can also serve as strong reminders, both to those who live in the home and to those who are visiting, of the presence of the saints and the nearness of heaven. There are also countless stories about a well-placed Miraculous Medal being effective in converting hearts.

Humor and Lightheartedness

Humor and a light heart are also essential tools, and like honey, they attract. These two elements can help in almost any situation and just make people want to be around you. Popular culture repeatedly vilifies clergy (particularly members of Opus Dei à la *The Da Vinci Code*) and anyone remotely religious by characterizing them as dour, angry, and emotionally repressed. Living contrary to this ridiculous model is likely to raise the eyebrows of people who have never really been around a faithful Catholic.

One of the things I most appreciate about being around fellow Catholics is that the humor is deeply entertaining and creative; anything crass or insensitive generally doesn't get shared. John Paul II is also known to have had a keen sense of humor. Shortly after his death in April 2005, the wife of a deceased Secret Service agent told me a story about the pope that she didn't want to be lost to time. She said her husband had been on duty when the Polish pope said Mass at St. Matthew's Cathedral in Washington, D.C., and for a luncheon that followed at the rectory next door. After the meal the young pope followed the Secret Service agent down a back flight of stairs. Rather than walk, the pope hoisted himself upon the banister and slid down, falling into the arms of the stunned agent at the bottom of the stairs. The pope, cracking himself up, simply smiled and said, "Secret Service, ha ha ha," and then went on with business as usual, as if nothing had happened.

Not every form of humor is edifying, however. During my teenage and college years, my immediate family related to each other through wit and sarcasm. While it kept all of us laughing, there was usually someone who didn't appreciate being the subject of the joke. A friend of mine, finally tired of my witticisms made at his expense, told me as much. It had never occurred to me that my sharp comments could be wounding him so deeply. I decided to try to cut out the sarcasm for a while and see what happened. Very gradually, almost indiscernibly, a change came about in my relationships, especially with my family. We started to talk more and really listen to what the other was saying instead of trying to come up with something that would make all the others laugh. Our relationships grew deeper, our communications more genuine because we could finally let down our guard. When I worked as a waitress, I was taught that if you approached a table that was too loud, you should speak quietly to the customers and the whole table would usually quiet down. I can see that this is also exactly what happened in the case of sarcasm. When I turned down my own biting wit, so did everyone else. Like good hospitality, good humor should leave people feeling edified.

Know Your Limits: The Un-nudgeables

While certainly no one is beyond hope, there are always situations that we are not called to. Here is where discernment comes in again. We need to distinguish between those who are merely difficult to be with and those we truly should not be around. And we are not talking about people you think simply won't convert.

Toxic personalities, or "the un-nudgeables," is one category to avoid. I once had a friend, Phillip, who was a great conversationalist. He was well traveled, worked with names gracing magazines, and had a keen aesthetic sense. We spent a long time discussing religion and faith, and his lack of it. Over time, however, it became clear that he was very good at weaving together truths and untruths. After months of never quite being able to piece together his stories, I found myself very uneasy in his presence. Odd stories about him also surfaced from his colleagues. One day, driving to his office to drop something off, I was so anxious that I couldn't bring myself to stop. I knew there were just too many red flags to continue any sort of a relationship with him. Our friendship did not continue because of the clarity I had that his sincerity and good intentions could not be counted upon. Eventually I learned that Phillip had a serious substance abuse problem. It was a roadblock I wasn't called to tackle.

Frequently people have similar situations in families, where there are old wounds that just keep getting torn wide open when conflicts arise. Abusive relationships, codependency, and general ill will should be treated carefully with proper boundaries. While all things work for the good of those who love God, the Lord also expects us to use sound judgment to protect ourselves and our loved ones.

Another red-flag situation is "missionary dating," or dating someone in hopes that he or she will become Catholic once you fall in love with each other. While I have seen this work a time or two with some unique individuals, it generally doesn't go well because the faithful individual sacrifices too much of him- or herself, especially in our current dating culture, in which any boundaries are hard to come by. God doesn't yoke healthy and happy couples together with sin. He puts couples together who will build each other up and grow stronger in their faith together.

In these cases, as in all others, prayer is critical, both for the other person's soul and for your own wisdom in dealing with a difficult situation. Sometimes it's simply God's will that you walk away.

Trust and Give Them Back to God

It is important to remember that not everything relies upon you, but that conversions can be a long process involving a whole host of characters. You may, however, have a crucial role to play in the salvation of a soul, wittingly or not. And such a role is usually not played by the "extras" whose job is just to fill up space. Even if it is something as simple as prayer, start there.

Many times, however, our best-laid efforts don't have the effect we hoped for. "One of the more serious temptations which stifles boldness and zeal is a defeatism which turns us into querulous and disillusioned pessimists, 'sourpusses,'" Pope Francis explains. "Nobody can go off to battle unless he is fully convinced of victory beforehand."[10]

The pope warns, "The evil spirit of defeatism is brother to the temptation to separate, before its time, the wheat from the weeds; it is the fruit of an anxious and self-centered lack of trust."[11] Keep in mind that your efforts are part of God's greater plan. He is in charge. It is all on his time. Any attachments you have to the outcome will generally lead to frustration and disappointment, while harming your own trust in God.

"While painfully aware of our own frailties," the Argentine pope continues, "we have to march on without giving in, keeping in mind what the Lord said to St. Paul: 'My grace is sufficient for you, for my power is made perfect in weakness'" (2 Corinthians 12:9).[12] Even when our efforts don't bear the fruits we expect, we must trust that God, who loves those we love more than we ever could, knows what he is doing. We must continually give these souls back to him, freeing them through forgiveness of any anger, fear, sadness, or frustration that we might feel toward them and lifting them back to him without our earthly strings and expectations attached.

Four

SUFFERING AND SACRIFICE

Mary was the ninety-two-year-old woman I met after Mass, first mentioned in the Introduction, who inspired the writing of this book. While lamenting her five faithless daughters, she also bemoaned her two artificial hips, which were wearing out. "Do you offer up the pain for your daughters?" I asked. "Oh, no," she said. "I usually just complain about them." What Mary and most of us forget too readily is the pure spiritual gold we have in the array of pains we experience in our daily lives.

While most of us complain about our struggles, or avoid them as best we can, the saints offer a much different picture of the real value of suffering. They repeatedly emphasize the hard spiritual currency that suffering is when united with Christ for winning souls, bringing healing, atoning for sin, and averting evil. St. Vincent de Paul once said, "If we only knew the precious treasure hidden in infirmities, we would receive them with the same joy with which we receive the greatest benefits, and we would bear them without ever complaining or showing signs of weariness."[1]

We have all heard the line "offer it up," perhaps so many times that it seems trite, but why do we dismiss its spiritual truth? Perhaps one reason is that it is difficult to actually see what happens with those aches and pains we give back to God. There is something enigmatic about suffering; we can't fully see or understand the fruits of it.

Shortly after Pope Benedict XVI abdicated the papacy but before the election of Pope Francis, my three-year-old daughter badly sprained her elbow. Before she went to sleep, I encouraged her to offer her pain to God for the new pope. She said a little prayer, as only a three-year-old can, and then she looked at me and asked: "Mommy, what is the new pope going to do with a silly old boo-boo?" Her question, while bringing a smile to my face and making me realize how much more explaining I needed to do, got to the point: It is just hard to know what God is going to do with a boo-boo, any boo-boo.

Discussing suffering and our own sacrifices in relationship to conversions is difficult, however, both because of the mystery of it and because of the way our own sacrifices help us while simultaneously helping others. It is difficult to speak of them separately. St. Paul makes it clear, however, that suffering has a real connection to the growth of the Church. "Now I rejoice in my sufferings for your sake, and in my flesh I complete what is lacking in Christ's afflictions for the sake of his body, that is, the church" (Colossians 1:24). It is in suffering that we best mimic the love of Christ by pouring ourselves out for others in the most selfless of gifts.

One way to think about suffering in relationship to self and neighbor is to look at the different phases of the spiritual life. Herein the different types of suffering people experience can be seen, particularly their relative fruitfulness, based upon each soul's relationship to God.

The first stage involves the pain of an individual who has no relationship with God, what I call "suffering *from* self." The second stage comes when the soul turns to God, a penance stage in which the pain suffered is largely in atonement for one's own sins, a "suffering *for* self." And finally the third stage is when the soul has reached a point where it understands that love mimics Christ and his outpouring of self, "suffering for others." This stage, as one might imagine, is the most fruitful when the soul prays for conversions. Interestingly, these pains can be related to the Church's teaching on hell, purgatory, and heaven.

Suffering from Self: Hell

As a college student I spent several months in Avignon, France, which had been the seat of the French papacy during the thirteenth century. Still early in my own conversion, I knew that the Palace of the Popes was a special place, so I decided to spend twenty minutes there every weekday in between classes. Somewhere I had read the recommendation by St. John Vianney to sit quietly and look at God while letting him look at me. It was my first effort at contemplative prayer, although I didn't know that was what it was at the time. I just wanted to know God, so it seemed to be a place to start.

After many months of doing this, I recall having very clear insights into how much people suffered from their own sins—not a miraculous vision, just a clear knowledge through reason that so many of the world's social ills could be solved if people simply started living the Ten Commandments. I wondered how I hadn't seen it before.

Unfortunately, much suffering is self-inflicted, wittingly or not. The pain of sin is unique because not only is it not fruitful in helping others, it is the exact opposite; the effects of sin and the accompanying pain get passed along to those in its wake.

Often we are surrounded by those who have yet to find God in their lives. These people can be difficult to journey with through life because there is a type of suffering unique to sin, a suffering that can never be fruitful or joyful. It is an introverted, self-absorbing kind of pain that at times seems to provide no way out because of its self-perpetuating nature. One sin seems to lead to another.

As most of us have experienced, sin—any sin, but particularly mortal sin—is accompanied by some kind of pain. It can be seen in broken relationships, weakness of character, wounded offspring, addiction, etc. Regardless of our intentions, sin is going to hurt. The hurt is built right into the package on purpose. God allows the pain as a warning to us that something we are doing isn't right, so even if the conscience fails, the pain should be a helpful clue. Suffering is God's meat tenderizer, pounding out our hard hearts, which have been turned to stone by pride, sin, indifference, vanity, etc. At some point, one hopes and prays, the soul will sit up and say, "Enough!"

There is frequently a painful bridge between this first suffering, suffering *from* self, and the second kind, suffering *for* self, which will be dealt with in the next section. It often comes in the form of "hitting rock bottom." This is not just for addicts involved with twelve-step programs, but for those of us who live faithlessly. Sin has blinded us to the reality of our own littleness and the enormity of God's love for us as his children. For those open to his grace, the experience of hitting rock bottom can be used by God to clarify our vision of reality. Through it God can simultaneously tear down and build up.

Jake was a young man with the world at his fingertips. Nearing the end of his doctoral studies in psychology, he was intoxicated with the theories of his field. Openly mocking and belittling the faith that had been passed along to him by his parents, he made it clear that he saw religion as terribly outmoded. Somehow, however, everything soured. A few of his female professors decided they didn't like him because of his outspoken and masculine approach to their field. His grades suffered because of his professors' sexism, and he was also passed over two years in a row for a critical internship, leaving him unemployable in his field.

Those two-plus years were enough to take the wind out of Jake's sails and lead him to reevaluate his whole life, especially this pedestal upon which he had put his profession. He moved back in with his parents and lived in a sort of limbo, waiting for the next opportunity to come along to get started with his professional life—but that limbo, through pain and time, was enough to bring him to his knees and allow him to find his faith once more.

Alcoholics Anonymous makes it very clear that most alcoholics will not change until they reach some sort of rock bottom when they realize that they are completely out of control of their lives. It is at that point that the twelve steps can have their positive effect. The wisdom of any twelve-step program, however, is not limited simply to addictions. Fr. Emmerich Vogt, a Dominican working out of Washington State, had made great headway in service to the Church by applying the twelve steps to the spiritual life. Many of us have to get to that point where we realize we are not in control—God is, and we need to get in line with him if we ever expect any sort of happiness in our lives.

As an outsider, watching a loved one hit rock bottom can be incredibly difficult, particularly if one is in a position to cushion the landing through financial means or otherwise. But this is also where trust comes in once we have discerned that it is better not to enable destructive behavior. As every parent knows, it is difficult to watch even minor occasions of self-inflicted pain, but at some point we have to let go and let our loved ones grow beyond themselves.

Suffering for Self: Purgatory

The second stage of suffering is, by necessity, for ourselves. We must make amends for what we have broken. So many saints speak of the tears they have wept as they recollect their own sinfulness. This awareness itself, though painful, is a great grace.

The suffering of a repentant soul is where the fruitful kind of suffering can begin—where we are no longer tearing our lives down, but building them up within God's grace. This kind of suffering, however, is not something we can skip over. In one form or another, reparation has to be made. Some of it may not be obvious, and there isn't really a clear line to indicate that your penance is finished, but it is necessary to give back our daily suffering, large or small, to repair what we have broken (or left in ruins). This is not to say that prayers for others cannot be offered during this spiritual stage; just that the necessity of suffering for oneself still exists.

Romans 5:3–4 offers another glimpse into the fruit of suffering: "We also rejoice in our sufferings, because we know that suffering produces perseverance; perseverance, character; and character, hope." This is one of the problems with the Protestant formulation of "being saved." It doesn't recognize that there is still hard work to do to clean up the mess one has made. Once again, twelve-step programs offer insights into this reality, because several of the steps include making specific reparation and offering apologies when still possible.

Most of us tread spiritual water in this stage, largely because we simply don't want to suffer. We like our comforts, and the thought of suffering can be daunting. Regardless of our thoughts on suffering, the obstacles to our learning how to love will be roughed out somewhere, either on earth through our own efforts (and the Holy Spirit's) or in purgatory, where we can't do anything to merit progress, but must rely upon the prayers and sacrifices of others.

The Church, in her gentle approach, offers ways to get used to suffering, including recommended weekly fasts, tithing, almsgiving, and other suggested sacrifices. Slowly these sorts of offerings can take deeper root and open the door to the third stage, suffering for others.

A priest I know taught me to try to look at every daily complaint, including getting cut off in traffic, being woken up countless times a night by children, and every ache and pain of the body, as an avenue to holiness. I like to joke with my husband on the rare occasion that he is irritating me by saying: "You are making me really holy right now." Invariably it makes us laugh, but it is a good way to remind myself of the true road to holiness.

Suffering for Others: Heaven

Years ago I was suffering deeply from an emotional wound. One afternoon my dearest friend and I were supposed to meet, but Kathy called to say that she couldn't make it because she had just sprained her ankle and couldn't walk. After making sure she had help at hand, I decided to go spend some time in Adoration. While there, I felt the Holy Spirit tell me that Kathy had sprained her ankle for me, to help heal my heart. Although I had no way of proving if it really was the case, I found the idea consoling and shared it with her as an encouragement in her pain.

Months passed and my emotional wound gradually healed. It wasn't, however, until about six months later that I thought about Kathy's sprained ankle again. I met the man who is now my husband, and during our courtship he told me about how he had fractured his ankle, not more than a week after Kathy had sprained hers. My future husband was still wearing an air cast because of the severity of the break. After putting the ankle stories and their timing together, I felt more convinced than ever that both ankles really were the source of healing for my wounded heart. Whom else would God ask to suffer for me than my closest friend and the man who had the most to gain from my healing? My husband's sacrifices for me started before we had even met.

What differentiates the suffering of penance from suffering for others is the gift of self. St. Thomas Aquinas wisely wrote, "The affection of charity in one who suffers on behalf of a friend makes greater satisfaction to God than if he suffered on behalf of himself; suffering for others is prompted by charity but suffering for self is prompted by necessity."[2]

According to the saints suffering has much more to offer than penance. St. Faustina, the scribe of *Divine Mercy*, wrote, "Suffering is a great grace; through suffering the soul becomes like the Savior; in suffering love becomes crystallized; the greater the suffering, the purer the love."[3] Suffering is the classroom of pure love, through which we come to be more like Christ.

Ironically suffering for others can have the appearance of hell, though all who practice it are closest to heaven. And yet despite the pain, even when it's disfiguring and ugly, when these souls know they are offering a great gift back to God, they live with great joy.

It is in offering ourselves for the lives of others through all of our discomforts that conversions are brought about most efficiently. Moreover Scripture makes clear that certain sins can be removed only through prayer, almsgiving, and fasting.

As a soul progresses in the spiritual life and toward a truer love of Christ, many describe experiencing the same trials experienced by our Savior: difficult journeys, false accusations, ridicule, disdain, even the stigmata. Rather than being signs of disfavor, when our pains mimic Christ's, they are sure road signs that we are on the right path. Experiencing a particularly difficult trial, St. Teresa of Ávila is noted to have said to our Lord, "If this is how you treat your friends, no wonder you have so few of them." And yet this is exactly how our Lord treats his friends. It is only through him, through his cross, that suffering can come to make any sense. Many misguided philosophies have tried to ignore suffering or explain it away, but only by embracing it can we come to understand its power as love.

Joy and Gratitude in Suffering

Christ tells his disciples not to let others know when they are fasting or giving alms. "Do not look gloomy" (Matthew 6:16), and "when you give alms, do not let your left hand know what the right is doing" (Matthew 6:3). These things should be done in secret, and with joy.

Pope Francis, acknowledging the difficulty of finding joy while suffering, warns that "[t]here are Christians whose lives seem like Lent without Easter." He explains, "I realize of course that joy is not expressed the same way at all times in life, especially at moments of great difficulty. Joy adapts and changes, but it always endures, even as a flicker of light born of our personal certainty that, when everything is said and done, we are infinitely loved."[4] Joy while enduring suffering, the pope goes on to say, is really built upon a "quiet yet firm trust" in our Lord, even in great distress.[5]

In addition to building firm trust, we can find joy more easily if we have a sense of humor. Lindsay, a young mother with a difficult father-in-law, offered up her pregnancy-related hemorrhoids for her husband's cantankerous father. "He makes it easy to remember who that pain is for," she quipped.

Frequently, when people look back on their lives, they are very grateful for the pain and struggles, even if they didn't see God's providence through them at the time. I used to carry a quote from an unknown source around in a prayer book as a reminder of how God has used great injuries to an even greater effect: "A salve so wonderful was applied to the wound that it made one positively grateful for the injury."

It is always difficult to be mindful of the fruit of suffering and to live with its hope, but that is where trust and faith grow and live.

Five

ASK QUESTIONS

When I was in college, I went on a date with the dreamiest (or so I thought) man. Doug was from the East Coast, with classic chiseled features and a fancy undergraduate degree—all very exotic to a young woman in Eugene, Oregon. As we drove to the Oregon coast, he started asking me questions about the area: who the first settlers were, the history of particular spots, and local lore. I didn't have a single answer for him, despite the fact that I had spent many vacations at the beach and only lived an hour away. At one point after I was unable to come up with anything interesting to say about the area, Doug jokingly asked, "Do you know anything?" I just smiled, but I knew he was onto something. I didn't really pay much attention to the world around me. I was comfortable in my daily life and wasn't interested in ideas and history beyond the requirements for my college courses. Spurred on by pride, I decided that day that I didn't want to be a ditzy girl, that I would pay more attention to everything. Ultimately my own interests caught flame, and the pride was replaced by a real thirst for knowledge and truth. I suspect Doug would be astounded to know the effect his simple question had upon my whole life.

We often underestimate the power of regular conversations, over coffee or a meal, to change the hearts of loved ones and strangers. Pope Francis has pointed out that there is an "informal preaching which takes place in the middle of a conversation . . ."[1] Often, however, we are so busy sharing about ourselves that we overlook an important tool used with precision over and over by Christ throughout the Gospels: engaging the other person through asking questions.

Spending any amount of time with small children will demonstrate the power of questions. Why? Why? Why? I wish I had a dollar for every "Why?" my children ask and the string of whys that follow it. The whys of children, however, seem to follow a similar pattern, like a Russian doll—they just keep asking, going deeper and deeper and deeper, and they show us how fundamental the quest for truth is to the human person.

Christ's Questions

The art of asking questions is nothing new. In Genesis 3:8–13, God asks Adam and Eve where they are, although of course he knows full well where they are and how they got there. The ancient Greek philosopher Socrates asked so many questions that he inspired an approach used to get at certain truths using questions: the Socratic method.

When most people consider the teachings of Christ, they likely think of the parable as his most favored tool. However, while harder to spot, Christ's more frequent tool was his use of questions. The Gospels are riddled with questions from Our Lord, especially in Matthew, where Jesus asks questions in nearly every chapter. Here are a few of the more famous:

> *"What profit is there for one to gain the whole world and forfeit his life?" (Mark 8:36)*

> *"Who is my mother? Who are my brothers?" (Matthew 12:48)*
>
> *"Who do people say that I am?" "But who do you say that I am?" (Mark 8:27, 29)*
>
> *"Why were you looking for me? Did you not know that I must be in my Father's house?" (Luke 2:49)*
>
> *"Who touched me?" (Luke 8:45)*
>
> *"Can any of you by worrying add a moment to your lifespan?" (Luke 12:25)*
>
> *"Woman, where are they? Has no one condemned you?" (John 8:10)*
>
> *"Woman, why are you weeping? Whom are you looking for?" (John 20:15)*

Jesus is also quoted several times answering a question with a question, especially when the Pharisees are trying to trip him up.

> *"Why do your disciples break the tradition of the elders? They do not wash [their] hands when they eat a meal." He said to them in reply, "And why do you break the commandment of God for the sake of your tradition?" (Matthew 15:2–3)*

Then they wanted his opinion:

> *"Is it lawful to pay the census tax to Caesar or not?" Knowing their malice, Jesus said, "Why are you testing me, you hypocrites? Show me the coin that pays the census tax." Then they handed him the Roman coin. He said to them, "Whose image is this and*

whose inscription?" They replied, "Caesar's." At that he said to them, "Then repay to Caesar what belongs to Caesar and to God what belongs to God." (Matthew 22:17–21)

Many of the questions are directed at Peter. You can almost see Peter bracing himself, like an unprepared student at the front of the class, as yet another series of questions comes his way.

"And he asked them, 'But who do you say that I am?' Peter said to him in reply, 'You are the Messiah.'" (Mark 8:29)

And much later, after his crucifixion Jesus presses Peter three times:

"Simon, son of John, do you love me?" (John 21:16)

All of these questions cannot be merely a rhetorical flourish. Instead it seems Jesus is showing us what an important tool they can be because questions force people to shift focus and look more deeply within themselves. Questions are like a mirror. They reflect to the questioner what he does and does not know. As Socrates made clear, questions sift out the truth. They make us think about things in a new and clearer way.

Like Christ with the Pharisees, questions shake us out of our tidy boxes of thought that we live in comfortably. Regrettably we don't have the advantage that Jesus did of knowing what is on the minds of those to whom we are speaking, but that shouldn't stop us from trying to help others find the truth with trust in the quiet assistance of the Holy Spirit. As Scripture says: "I planted, Apollos watered, but God caused the growth" (1 Corinthians 3:6).

Changing Hearts by Changing Minds

What I am proposing here is the exact opposite of apologetics (which will be discussed in chapter six). Instead of providing answers, you are the one drawing them out. Asking pointed questions can help someone discover new things, as opposed to directly telling someone something he or she didn't know. As any teacher can tell you, discoveries made by the student are a much more powerful way of learning than even the best spoon-fed insights.

The art of asking questions is not about what you think needs to be said, but about what needs to be asked to get to something deeper. The late famed journalist Robert Novak, speaking of his own conversion once said that he decided to become a Catholic after a young coed asked him what he thought would happen to him when he died. "We all die, you know," she insisted. He said he never had really thought about it until she asked him directly.

While you may not have to be as intense as Novak's coed, asking questions has a way of making people think about things not previously on their radar and reconsider their own basic assumptions. Even if someone gives a pat answer to a deep question, it may plant a seed. After the conversation, they may go back to it, like Novak, and rethink it.

Another benefit of questions is that they can be extremely appealing to the one being asked. There are very few people who do not like to be asked their opinion on an issue. While it could be pride in some, for most it is simply the desire to be known and loved by others, and this can't happen without being asked about what is inside.

Thomas O'Gorman, an Irish pro-life advocate who died tragically in 2014, offered a great model, according to his eulogy, of both loving people where they are at and getting to the heart of the issue with questions. "He had the ability to blend with younger people. He would happily sit and chat away with them for hours. He found common ground—sports or movies, a game of Uno. Then he would begin a discussion on the deeper questions that many young people have inside, but perhaps do not get a chance to talk about."[2]

Questions can also be used very effectively on topics that are difficult to debate; a well-placed question can jostle any mind by recasting the issue. John was an engineer and used to finding very good practical solutions to problems. Somewhere during his life, he had been taught that abortion was a very good way of resolving a lot of problems. It just made sense to his engineering mind. That is, until his brother, James, asked him some questions, without guile or bitterness. "What's so magic about the second or third trimester? Or, for that matter, birth? Sure, it's a wonderful thing, but how does the child so fundamentally change that mothers aren't allowed to do one day what they could the day before? And why can't parents be allowed to do when the child is six or eight what they are allowed to do when she is six or eight weeks in the womb?" To John's credit, he returned to James's questions over and over for more than a year. One day he simply announced, "You're right, James; some solutions just aren't right. Abortion can't be the answer."

Questions, when used properly, don't have to be like swords; they can be invitations to find something hidden, something true. Combined with authentic love and charity for the person you are engaging, questions are powerful tools.

Some Sample Questions:

Why?
What do you think?
Do you ever feel like something is missing in your life?
What do you want your life to have looked like when you are eighty years old?

Why do you go to X church?

Why don't you go to church?

What do you think the reason for life is?

Do you pray?

As this list reveals, even the most basic questions can get to the heart of the matter without being complicated (or conniving).

When Silence Is Golden

The art of asking questions also involves the art of listening. Nothing can be more deflating to a conversation than feeling like you are not really being listened to. We all share a deep desire as human beings to be known and loved by others.

If listening is difficult for you, keep these things in mind: Focus, be attentive, make eye contact, put away your phone. If you are at a party, don't watch the door to see who has just arrived. Just listen. Think of yourself as a detective. Often there are clues in a person's responses—in what is said, what is not said, and in the way it is said (or not said). These clues can lead to other questions, or can give you insights into the roadblocks someone is dealing with. But these can't be discovered if you are not paying attention.

If talking too much is your weakness, this is a good time to practice patience and just keep your mouth shut. If you are cynical, leave those responses at the door and simply let your friend answer; avoid clobbering him with the response. Nothing extinguishes wonder and joy like the weight of cynical comments.

Also be mindful of how someone is responding to your arguments or discussions. I recall talking to my brother about the faith over a beer one night when we were both fresh out of college. He was slowly making his way back to the Church, and I was doing my best to help him. After a while he told me, as only a brother can, that he'd had his fill of our discussion and we needed to talk about something else. "You're beginning to look like Dad when he would lecture us," he chided. I try to remember to keep a check on my own zeal, avoiding the "fire hose effect" when I do have the ear of someone seeking the truth. A few words can go a long way; sometimes further than many words.

If you are like me, the pithy response I wish I had given always eludes me until well after it is useful. Asking questions avoids that issue because sometimes the best response is no response, leaving your interlocutor to stew on his or her own thoughts, again with the quiet assistance of the Holy Spirit, instead of latching on to yours.

In the end the virtues of prudence and discernment are vital for knowing when to be silent and when to speak; when to ask something deeper and when to go back to something superficial; and when to ask questions and when to jump in when it is clear someone needs a little guidance.

Making Room to Talk

Before mass media, there were plenty of opportunities for asking questions and having edifying conversations. Our culture, with its abhorrence of silence, fills in many of the blanks that used to be there when spending time chatting with people. It is for this reason that we have to work that much harder to create space to just talk—and talk beyond sports, TV shows, and family matters.

My husband had a friend, Jason, who, when he was very sick with cancer, asked some others to go to a museum with him. Having very little in common with them intellectually, Jason set some ground rules for their visit. Knowing this was perhaps one of their last outings with him, the others happily obliged. The main rule was, no one could make any meaningless comments about a work of art. No "This is nice," or "Wow," or "Interesting" allowed. Any comments had to have some substance, even if it was to recall a memory, make a tangential point, or ask a question. What Jason was doing was carving out space to talk, to really engage in a topic instead of simply gliding along the surface of life.

I have found that dinner parties in particular, especially if kept to ten people or fewer, are ripe for real discussions. My husband and I once hosted a dinner party with a total of five couples and asked each person to bring one idea for a topic they would like to discuss. Everything was on the table for discussion: culture, beauty, art, philosophy, a book they were reading, a theological debate, etc. The idea was just to get people together to have a real conversation and not to default to small talk: How was your week? How is work? How are the children? How are your parents? Did you see the game? We wanted our guests to think seriously about something beyond the day-to-day and to see what is real in our lives beyond the dictates of our screens and the daily news cycle.

Even something as simple as starting a fire and watching the flames dance, going for a drive, reading a passage from a book, or playing a game together can go a long way toward carving out space for real conversations—and real conversions.

Six

NO EVANGELIZATION WITHOUT EDUCATION

The Acton Institute in Grand Rapids, Michigan, has a unique problem. It can't seem to keep Protestants on staff. No, staff members don't drive Protestants from the workplace. They convert them. There is nothing forced about these conversions; it is just that this think tank, full of zealous converts and cradle Catholics, engages in a lot of lively and open conversation about Christianity. At a certain point the Protestants find the Catholic arguments just too compelling to stay comfortably in their non-Catholic denominations. The combined weight of theology, history, the organic unity of the Church's doctrines, and the example of men and women striving to live their faith is just too compelling.

Unfortunately most of us don't live or work in an environment that conveys the bounty of our faith. If only all of us lived in such a rich atmosphere of education, conversation, discussion, and discovery! This is the ideal that universities, particularly those in the liberal arts, were set up to be. And yet we now know education in general to be, more often than not, the antithesis of this model of wonder, enrichment, and truth.

The absence of authentic education has left a void that has been filled by sloppy reasoning, sappy and empty emotionalism, and a prevailing attitude of malaise and cynicism. Our faith, however, has so much more to offer all of us.

Pope Francis reminds us that all people are thirsting for truth and that, as Catholics, we need to address every need of the human heart. "Unless these people find in the Church a spirituality which can offer healing and liberation, and fill them with life and peace, while at the same time summoning them to fraternal communion and missionary fruitfulness, they will end up being taken in by solutions which neither make life truly human nor give glory to God."[1] As the pope makes clear, the Church has the solutions to the hungers of the human heart.

One of the reasons for the success of the folks at Acton is the beauty of the unity of ideas that make up Catholic doctrine and theology. There is no contradiction within the faith. While there are clearly mysteries that are difficult to explain, such as the Trinity, two thousand years of experience and theology have provided a rich context for conveying the Church's truths.

Pope Francis discusses this "organic unity" among the truth of our faith:

> *The integrity of the Gospel message must not be deformed. What is more, each truth is better understood when related to the harmonious totality of the Christian message; in this context all of the truths are important and illumine one another.*[2]

For example, it is for this reason that Pope John Paul II was able to write so nimbly about a theology of the body. Sexuality and moral teaching are woven together. There is moral consistency. The bigger issue seems to be that people simply don't know it.

There are two trends happening among those converting. The first is that Catholics who know very little about the faith are *leaving* it for community offered by Protestant churches. Meanwhile, well-educated Protestants are *joining* the Catholic faith because their research continually points back to Catholicism. Scott Hahn, Jeff Cavins, and the late Fr. Richard John Neuhaus are a few such souls.

Looking at these trends it is clear that we need to do a better job of catechizing those within the faith, who are looking for community and fellowship but don't realize exactly what it is they are giving up—communion with Christ through the Eucharist and other sacraments. These two trends offer clues as to how best to reach someone in either camp.

Starting in the Pews: Belief Seeking Understanding

"No one has ever told me this before," the young woman said with incredulity. "Why didn't I know that the Church teaches X? I've gone to Catholic school my whole life!"

This is the all-too-frequent refrain of so many Catholics when they hear the truth about nearly every controversial tenet of the Catholic faith. Unfortunately the 70s and 80s were very bad years for teaching the faith. Even now we still have a long way to go to regain all that was lost for the average person in the pew after the chaos that ensued after the Second Vatican Council.

On any given Sunday, it has been reported, 95 percent of the Catholics in the pews will be using or supporting contraception, despite the Church's firm conviction that contraception is a grave mortal sin. And huge percentages of them, not knowing any better, will also receive Communion. While going into how we got these scandalously high numbers is a topic for another book, the reality is that we as Catholics are faced with a spectrum of people who need our help. Most Catholics range from being simply uneducated to actually being miseducated about their Catholic faith, in that they do not know what the Church teaches, but they think they do and therefore reject whatever real teaching they have been presented. Regrettably most of those who fall on this end of the spectrum were educated in Catholic schools and lived through the post-Vatican II chaos, during which, as one woman said, answers to moral issues depended more upon the opinions of priest you spoke to instead of being sourced back to Scripture and/or Church teaching.

The bad news about this set of folks is that they already have deep-seated ideas and habits, which first must be uprooted or debunked before the right ones are replanted. This is no small task. As most mothers will tell you, it is considerably easier to give children something new to eat that they have never eaten than to give them something they have already tried but are convinced they don't like. As adults we can be the same way about long-held beliefs. How do you convince someone who has had years of misguided "Catholic" education that what they got wasn't really the truth? And yet that is what we are facing today because of the crisis of faith that hit the core of our Catholic institutions after the Second Vatican Council—not to say the council was the cause of it, but that was the reaction, from which the Church is still recovering.

The good news about this set of Catholics is that they usually have some actual belief in God; it just hasn't been tended to properly. St. Anselm, a medieval theologian and philosopher, spoke of faith seeking understanding *(fides quaerens intellectum)*. While Anselm's explanation of the idea is much more detailed than needs to be discussed here, suffice it to say that because this set of Catholics have some actual foundational belief, it is a good place to start. The tougher issue is to break through to this faith with fresh ideas about orthodoxy. Often, the biggest impediment to reaching these souls is general ignorance of

Church teaching, which can lead to sin, such as intellectual pride and stubbornness, laziness (sloth), or a moral issue that someone may not be willing to confront. Seeing this difference makes it easier to know where to start when trying to help them see more clearly.

Max was an uneducated Catholic. As a college student he had been in a long-term relationship with Jennifer. As the years passed he began to become uncomfortable with the fact that they were sexually active. Having been raised a Catholic, he knew that premarital sex wasn't right, but he didn't know why. His unease led him to ask a priest at his local Newman Center. "Oh, those rules are a bit outdated," said the priest. "They were really in place just to protect women, but we don't really need them anymore." Feeling like he had done his due diligence, Max continued with the status quo. Shortly thereafter he was given the CD *Contraception: Why Not* by Janet Smith. It changed his life in one evening. Suddenly he got it. Over time his relationship with Jennifer fizzled out because the two just couldn't reconcile Max's new belief that premarital sex was really wrong, and because his aha moment with sexuality had opened his mind to other realities that he'd always assumed the Church got wrong. "If they are so right about this, what else have I been missing?" So Max searched. And he found. Learning the authentic Church teaching on one issue was a key that started to unlock so many other doors to his growing faith.

Many people are like Max. They just need to find the truth about the Church's teaching on one topic, and suddenly those other issues don't seem as outdated, prudish, medieval, or odd.

There are also plenty of Catholics who, when initially hearing the truth about the faith, just don't get it. It is so opposed to their own way of thinking that it doesn't make sense. Rich, though raised Catholic, found nothing of value in the faith as an adult; he found a lot more meaning in travel, women, and beer. His brother Andrew, who had spent years studying theology, moved in with him for several months. During their time together the two brothers talked a lot. It was clear that Rich thought Andrew's deep faith was a bit nuts, but Andrew didn't give up. He just kept planting seeds and stringing them together in a logical way. It wasn't until several years later that Rich realized how much his brother had informed his thoughts. Little by little what once were crazy ideas now seemed the most rational way to look at life. He went from being someone who only went to church on Christmas and Easter to being a weekly communicant, donating significant time and labor to his parish.

The sudden surge of Catholics taking advantage of new media is making the work of educating souls in this camp significantly easier. Having access to videos, articles, podcasts, and e-books, particularly when passed along through friends via Facebook, Instagram, etc., takes the effort out of passing around printed material or loaning DVDs (or VHS tapes). Moreover, students of all ages are no longer limited just to what their teachers teach or priests preach. It is easier now than ever to do our own research on a given topic, particularly if something doesn't sound quite right.

And while new media has its limits because some ideas simply can't be packaged into a sound bite, it goes a long way in providing the keys that can help unlock a renewed interest in the faith. "Let us never forget," the pope reminds us, "that the expression of truth can take different forms. The renewal of these forms of expression becomes necessary for the sake of transmitting to the people of today the Gospel message in its unchanging meaning."[3]

Old-School Apologetics

Apologetics, of course, aren't just for poorly catechized Catholics, but for everyone, particularly those with a lively intellectual life. There are many different types of people who fit into this category. Using reason, they are, wittingly or not, finding a belief in God for the first time or finding the Catholic faith. Their situation can be summarized as "understanding seeking the Catholic faith." There is an abundance of conversion stories chronicling these much more dramatic types of conversions from atheism or vehemently anti-Catholic Protestants. Many of these converts initially bristled at the idea of becoming Catholic, some kicking and screaming at the place their own research had brought them. One convert, a young man who had been preparing to be a Baptist minister, said that he couldn't stress enough how much he hated the idea of becoming Catholic. Only after time and a growing inner conviction of the truthfulness of the Catholic Church do these converts cross the Tiber. Often it comes at great expense, severing many relationships, scholarships, opportunities, and jobs.

Then there are others who hope that through reading and learning, faith will materialize and end their restless searching. When I was in graduate school studying philosophy at Franciscan University of Steubenville, I met one student who, for many reasons, stood out among the rest of us. Alex was one of these souls searching for truth, leaving no rock left unturned. Somehow this atheist from Oregon had found his way to Steubenville. Having studied philosophy in the analytic tradition, which is very logical and cerebral, he was always asking tight and pointed questions that left us all scratching our heads. I recall having long conversations with Alex that often left me frustrated because I didn't have good answers to his questions, though they led me to look for better responses. The other students and I, our professors, and the leaders of RCIA did our best to help him find peace in his restless soul.

After attending RCIA for his second year in a row, with Easter fast approaching, Alex was still unsure if he was joining the Church. Four days before the Easter Vigil, when he was supposed to be baptized, he told me the crushing news that he was going to wait yet another year to be baptized. I knew how agonizing the decision had been for him; after years of really wanting something solid to stand upon, he simply hadn't gotten to that point where he could believe in God.

The morning of the vigil, Holy Saturday, I went to lunch with Alex, his parents, who were in town for his scheduled baptism, and his potential godparents. While it was nice to be together, a cloud hung over us all (except for his parents, who were indifferent to his conversion). And then, after our meal, Alex made his announcement. Pulling out a copy of the Nicene Creed, he explained that he realized that he really *did* believe in every single one of its precepts. His ability to say, "Yes, I believe," to every assertion of the Creed removed his earlier doubts about God. He was coming into the Church after all.

For all of these types of individuals of various backgrounds, no sound bite will be compelling. There is a much deeper wrestling going on in the soul, a much deeper searching that might involve new media, but might also involve plenty of old media—books out of print, languages no longer spoken, and stories long forgotten. And it might involve a lot of conversations and witnessing by others to bring them around fully to all the Church has to give. This type of apologetics just takes time and prayer.

Not Just for Professionals

Starting with the basics every Catholic should be able to defend his or her faith, particularly on the more controversial issues of the day. "All the baptized, whatever their position in the Church or their level of instruction in the faith," writes Pope Francis, "are agents of evangelization, and it would be insufficient to envisage a plan of evangelization to be carried out by professionals while the rest of the faithful would simply be passive recipients."[4]

An advanced degree in theology isn't necessary. What is necessary is the ability to respond beyond a shrug and a blank stare. Sometimes this can even be as simple as knowing who has the answers. For example, Professor Janet Smith is the go-to expert on contraception, Catholic Answers has great responses to questions about the faith, and Fr. Robert Barron has a beautiful and compelling video series on Church history and theology.

Pope Francis warns us not to wait to join in the work of evangelization until we have it all figured out:

> *Of course, all of us are called to mature in our work as evangelizers. We want to have better training, a deepening love and a clearer witness to the Gospel. In this sense, we ought to let others be constantly evangelizing us. But this does not mean that we should postpone the evangelizing mission; rather, each of us should find ways to communicate Jesus wherever we are. All of us are called to offer others an explicit witness to the saving love of the Lord, who despite our imperfections offers us his closeness, his word and his strength, and gives meaning to our lives.*[5]

Apologetics can even be as simple as sharing a good book. The lives of the saints, as St. Ignatius of Loyola can attest, are always a good place to start when someone begins an inquiry into the faith. Ignatius had been a proud nobleman, wounded in battle. During his convalescence, as he lay bored in bed, he asked for something to read. The only books available were on the lives of saints. Reading these transformed his life and seeded his own faith, a faith that eventually led to his founding the Jesuit Order.

The saints' lives can be very effective, especially if you have a few of your favorites in mind. Set in a context removed from our own, saints' biographies are disarming—they don't seem to be tangled up in the same political and social dramas—while also offering surgical insights that lengthy catechesis cannot always convey. Sanctity is timeless; reading their lives reminds us of that. So often it is easy to feel like a good person when comparing yourself to all you see in the news, but reading the lives of the saints strips us of those delusions in a noncombative way.

Regardless of our efforts Pope Francis warns that certain care has to be taken to not make faith formation about scoring ideological points, or simply about doctrines. If we remove the actual relationship between man and God, something critical is missing. "It would mean that it is not the Gospel which is being preached, but certain doctrinal or moral points based on specific ideological options. The message will run the risk of losing its freshness and will cease to have 'the fragrance of the Gospel.'"[6]

While we can become comfortable in our own faith, the world around us is longing for answers to all the thorny issues of the faith. These issues are not just about politics, or rubrics of the faith, but go to the heart of every human being—to our relationship with God and with others and to the source of authentic happiness. The withholding of these ideas has led to what Mother Teresa described as the greatest poverty in our world: loneliness. No Christian should ever feel alone. Our Lord has promised that he is always with us. And yet so many of us are lonely, depressed, bored, angry, and enslaved by the very things our culture promises will make us happy. The truth is that the sacramental and authentic relationships with the Trinity and those put into our lives are what give us real freedom and a true foretaste of heaven on earth.

Give Your Best; God Will Do the Rest

Famed quarterback Philip Rivers, of the San Diego Chargers, recently told the graduates of the Catholic University of America in Washington, D.C., that before he leaves home to play in a football game, he and his wife pray a Hail Mary together, and then she says to him as he walks out the door, "Do your best and God will do the rest."

Pope John Paul II frequently encouraged everyone, especially the young, not to be satisfied with mediocrity. Often, we have the sense that if our intentions are good, that is enough. But is that truly giving our best? Just our best intentions? Giving our best means going beyond our own comfortable boundaries and not simply offering something mediocre and comfortable.

Picking up the same thread, Pope Francis adds,

> *In your heart you know that it is not the same to live without him; what you have come to realize, what has helped you to live and given you hope, is what you also need to communicate to others. Our falling short of perfection should be no excuse; on the contrary, mission is a constant stimulus not to remain mired in mediocrity but to continue growing.*[7]

In the immortal words of St. Ignatius of Loyola, "We must act as if everything depended on you; trust as if everything depended on God."[8]

Seven

CULTIVATE REAL CULTURE

As important as education and apologetics are, they are not enough. Unfortunately most people don't respond to tight and fine-tuned arguments. The abandonment of reason, which has been on the chopping block of our educational system for many decades, and the tyranny of niceness often make theological conversations an uncomfortable starting point for discussion.

Perhaps a better starting point in our own culture (with apologetics to follow) is to tap into the thirst we all have for meaning in our lives, the search for happiness or something deeper than many of the shallow realities we experience on a daily basis. We need to look for something more beyond argumentation. Authentic culture seems to be the key.

Culture is an abstract word that can often be hard to wrap one's head around. During the two years I spent researching it for a doctoral dissertation, I heard a wise priest articulate it very succinctly: "Culture is God's love made visible." After I let it sink in for a while, it occurred to me that what most consider historically the heights of culture in music, poetry, literature, clothing, architecture, and art are all beautiful. They are not tawdry, they do not denigrate the human person, and they aren't simply useful. They reflect God's love for us.

Culture, like all good gifts from God, is meant to be shared. No architect expects his work to be seen by just one person. No symphony practices tirelessly just for itself. Talents are gifts that God gives us to enjoy, but we enjoy them even more once they're shared. Every gift we have been given is meant not just for ourselves, but to be passed along to others. Culture is simply the manifestation of these gifts being shared.

Somehow over the past several centuries, the centrality to the Catholic faith of beauty, truth, and goodness—all elements that make up culture—has been lost from a collective consciousness about the Church and its history. It is an odd reality, if one thinks about it for very long, considering the churches, architecture, paintings, music, poetry, literature, and other important elements of material culture and style that have been crafted by Catholics living out their faith over the centuries. Think of Michelangelo, Fra Angelico, (Fr.) Vivaldi, Bach, Dante, Bernini, and Brunelleschi, to name a few.

Like a blank canvas, culture is a neutral expression; it takes on the characteristics of those who live in a given society. It can become something beautiful and compelling or something ugly and horrifying. I am convinced this is one of the reasons why people love Europe so much, because of the remnants of Catholic culture that abound. Much of Europe was built long ago, when people still had faith in God, and it is reflected certainly in the continent's churches, but also in the roadside grottoes one still sees in Poland and Greece or the ornately fashioned Madonnas nestled in the second-story corners of buildings, the medieval Latin phrases still inscribed on stone arcades or the sometimes capricious but always enthralling fountains in Paris and Rome. The list continues with the imagination, architectural feats, and breathtaking beauty of European churches, including the awe-inspiring soaring ceilings of

Chartres Cathedral, the embrace of St. Peter's Square, and the radiance of the stained glass at Sainte-Chapelle in Paris.

How, you may ask, does dwelling on culture involve conversions? Culture has the ability to reach the deepest recesses of a soul, to stir up something on a level never quite touched before. It is a reminder of the sublime, that which is beyond our mere humanity. The experience can conjure up something otherworldly but somehow familiar, which harkens the soul to dig deeper, to find more.

Author and Montessori teacher Sofia Cavalletti, in her book *The Religious Potential of the Child*, describes two types of classroom settings for educating preschool-age children using tactile materials to represent abstract ideas. The first set of materials was shallow and secular. When the day was finished, the child was tired, worn out, and cranky. The other setting was centered around the catechetical teaching on Christ the Good Shepherd. The same child left renewed, refreshed, and with a peaceful sense of contentedness. Time and again Cavalletti describes the joy of small children when given the right tools to soak up ideas about God. (One child, anxious to have more time with the materials, would turn forward the hands on a clock, tricking his mother into leaving for school early.)[1]

True culture, as an authentic reflection of God's love, isn't just for children. It has the potential to leave a similar imprint upon every soul: renewal, refreshment, and a peaceful sense of contentedness—all fingerprints of God's handiwork.

Culture may not trigger instantaneous conversion, but it serves to open the individual up to the gifts God has to offer and wants to offer in abundance. Convert Dietrich von Hildebrand, a philosopher who was hunted by Hitler before he found exile in the United States during World War II, often attributed his own conversion to his upbringing in Florence, Italy. As the son of an artist, von Hildebrand was raised with a deep appreciation for beauty of all forms: music, architecture, language, and the material arts. Later he met philosopher converts Edith Stein (St. Teresa Benedicta of the Cross) and Max Scheler. The force of their intellectual arguments and von Hildebrand's own ability to connect beauty to God as the divine artist made him a zealous convert.

The Way of Beauty

Pope Francis has called for people to evangelize the culture, doing it through that which "attracts." One Catholic has certainly answered his call. The 2014 season of the Italian talent show *The Voice of Italy* was rocked by a most unexpected contestant. The show starts with four musical coaches who sit in rotating chairs initially turned away from the performer, and if they like what they hear, they can turn their chair around to see the singer. Hearing a voice full of passion, verve, and beauty, the coaches never could have anticipated who was performing for them: a twenty-five-year-old Italian nun dressed in a plain black habit with a silver cross and dowdy black shoes, Sister Cristina Scuccia.

This talented nun with a light in her eyes had the coaches—pierced, tattooed, and boasting of wickedness—eating out of her hand. One became teary-eyed and confessed that he would be a saint if she had been singing at church when he was growing up. The motley group of coaches, who perhaps hadn't set foot in a church in some time, were clearly moved by her voice, which was complemented by her innocent energy and fearless effort to evangelize. Watching this out-of-place sister dancing and singing in her habit (especially without sound) looks more like a comedic skit than a real competition.

By the time she won the finale, Sister Cristina had groupies wearing T-shirts featuring her face. And yet if the coaches or audience had seen her on the street or met her under almost any other set of circumstances, her effect would have been lost. Her powerful voice and innocent spunk, contrasted with her out-of-place appearance, melted everyone's heart. From the beginning she made it clear that she wasn't after fame and fortune, but was simply responding to the call of Pope Francis to evangelize. Upon winning she led the audience in the Our Father.

Sister Cristina is the embodiment of the pope's words:

> *[W]e cannot forget that evangelization is first and foremost about preaching the Gospel to those who do not know Jesus Christ or who have always rejected him. Many of them are quietly seeking God, led by a yearning to see his face, even in countries of ancient Christian tradition. Instead of seeming to impose new obligations, they should appear as people who wish to share their joy, who point to a horizon of beauty and who invite others to a delicious banquet. It is not by proselytizing that the Church grows, but "by attraction.*[2]

Clearly Sister Cristina had found a way to share her joy, and it was infectious.

Popes John Paul II, Benedict XVI, and Francis have all spoken about the importance of beauty in the life of faith. While a discussion of beauty, truth, and goodness is nothing new, it is clear that these popes recognize the disparity between what the Church has taught about these essential elements and what is being lived out, particularly in the midst of the vapid relativism and nihilism that envelops modern culture.

Over the centuries what has been called "the way of beauty," or the *via pulchritudinis*, has served as a leaven to many an artisan, craftsman, and writer, not to mention the common man in the pew without any particular creative gifts. Pope Benedict likens the encounter with beauty to an open door to the infinite that goes beyond our daily routine.

Pope Benedict, a concert-quality pianist, explains further:

> *Perhaps it has happened to you at one time or another—before a sculpture, a painting, a few verses of poetry or a piece of music—to have experienced deep emotion, a sense of joy, to have perceived clearly, that is, that before you there stood not only matter—a piece of marble or bronze, a painted canvas, an ensemble of letters or a combination of sounds—but something far greater, something that "speaks," something capable of touching the heart, of communicating a message, of elevating the soul.*[3]

This elevation of the soul, Benedict explains, inspires prayer:

> *But there are artistic expressions that are true roads to God, the supreme Beauty—indeed, they are a help [to us] in growing in our relationship with him in prayer. We are referring to works of art that are born of faith, and that express the faith. We see an example of this whenever we visit a Gothic cathedral: We are ravished by the vertical lines that reach heavenward and draw our gaze and our spirit upward, while at the same time, we feel small and yet yearn to be filled.*[4]

Before Benedict, Pope John Paul II spoke of how beauty leads us to transcendence:

> *Beauty is a key to the mystery and a call to transcendence. It is an invitation to savour life and to dream of the future. That is why the beauty of created things can never fully satisfy. It stirs that hidden nostalgia for God which a lover of beauty like Saint Augustine could express in incomparable terms: "Late have I loved you, beauty so old and so new: late have I loved you!"*[5]

This experience of transcendence and wonder, the Polish pope explained, breeds a kind of enthusiasm that can save the world. "People of today and tomorrow need this enthusiasm if they are to meet and master the crucial challenges which stand before us. Thanks to this enthusiasm, humanity, every time it loses its way, will be able to lift itself up and set out again on the right path. In this sense it has been said with profound insight that "beauty will save the world."[6]

John Paul knew the power of art, having joined a troupe of actors during the dark years of German occupation of Poland during World War II. As the Germans tried to wipe out every vestige of Polish culture, the young Karol Wojtyla and his collaborators in the Rhapsodic Theater, risking death by firing squad if caught, performed plays to lift the hearts and minds of their select audiences in perhaps the darkest period of Polish history.

Following his predecessors Pope Francis recommends that all catechesis include not just truth but also beauty:

> *Every form of catechesis would do well to attend to the "way of beauty." Proclaiming Christ means showing that to believe in and to follow him is not only something right and true, but also something beautiful, capable of filling life with new splendour and profound joy, even in the midst of difficulties. Every expression of true beauty can thus be acknowledged as a path leading to an encounter with the Lord Jesus. This has nothing to do with fostering an aesthetic relativism which would downplay the inseparable bond between truth, goodness and beauty, but rather a renewed esteem for beauty as a means of touching the human heart and enabling the truth and goodness of the Risen Christ to radiate within it.*[7]

Kenneth Clark, a British art historian who converted to Catholicism on his deathbed, described the importance of beauty in his own life. He "had intuited . . . that truth and beauty are inextricably linked, and that one may lead us to the other. In the end he realised that our yearning for beauty is our yearning for God."[8]

Divine Creativity, Ever Fresh

Another feature of authentic culture is its freshness. The Trinity, being ancient and yet so new, as described by St. Augustine, gives creativity the hallmark of something new and inspiring, not boring and tired. "Jesus can also break through the dull categories with which we would enclose him and he constantly amazes us by his divine creativity," Pope Francis explains. "Whenever we make the effort to return to the source and to recover the original freshness of the Gospel, new avenues arise, new paths of creativity open up, with different forms of expression, more eloquent signs and words with new meaning for today's world. Every form of authentic evangelization is always 'new.'"[9] Not content with just a rehashing of what has been done in the past, Francis encourages us to find new ways to express ancient truths:

> *Each particular church should encourage the use of the arts in evangelization, building on the treasures of the past but also drawing upon the wide variety of contemporary expressions so as to transmit the faith in a new "language of parables." We must be bold enough to discover new signs and new symbols, new flesh to embody and communicate the word, and different forms of beauty which are valued in different cultural settings, including those unconventional modes of beauty which may*

mean little to the evangelizers, yet prove particularly attractive for others.[10]

Both John Paul and Benedict spoke eloquently of the authentic sources for inspiration. John Paul spoke of how it is the breath of the Holy Spirit breathed into the soul of the artist, while both spoke of the great depths of inspiration to be harvested from Scripture. "What Marc Chagall, a great artist, wrote," Pope Benedict explains, "remains profoundly true: that for centuries, painters dipped their paintbrush in that colored alphabet which is the Bible."[11] Pope John Paul expands the lens of influence the Bible has to include all artists:

Sacred Scripture has thus become a sort of "immense vocabulary" (Paul Claudel) and "iconographic atlas" (Marc Chagall), from which both Christian culture and art have drawn. The Old Testament, read in the light of the New, has provided endless streams of inspiration. From the stories of the Creation and sin, the Flood, the cycle of the Patriarchs, the events of the Exodus to so many other episodes and characters in the history of salvation, the biblical text has fired the imagination of painters, poets, musicians, playwrights and film-makers.[12]

Purpose, Order, and Discipline

Not all of us are called to be artists or creative. John Paul II, acknowledging this reality, reminds us that we have all been entrusted with the task of crafting our own lives. We are called to make our lives a work of art, carefully creating a masterpiece out of it.

And yet no work can be accomplished without purpose, order, and discipline. These are also crucial elements of authentic culture.

Catholicism has a rich history of bringing order out of chaos. When the Roman Empire was crumbling, the monastic system, established by St. Benedict, brought order and new life amid the ruins of Rome. The saint's emphasis upon rules and regimented time for prayer and work have spilled over into many other aspects of life beyond the monastic community.

It is the virtues and a sense of purpose and wonder that animate our desire for work. "A noted Polish poet," John Paul explained, "Cyprian Norwid, wrote that 'beauty is to enthuse us for work, and work is to raise us up.'"[13] Even if we are not making beautiful art, music, or poetry, our life's effort—our own masterpiece—can be something that inspires others. There is something intrinsically beautiful and attractive about a life well lived—a life ordered in virtue. A 1980s *Saturday Night Live* skit illuminates this reality by reminding the audience that beauty and order don't just crop up anywhere. The skit features award-winning poetry coming from prisons. Eddie Murphy portrays the most lauded of the artists, a convict with a life sentence who spends a lot of time in solitary confinement. He recites part of his poem titled "Images": "Dark and lonely on the summer night. Kill my landlord, kill my landlord. Watchdog barking—do he bite? . . . C-I-L-L my landlord."[14] The humor, of course, is that award-winning poetry doesn't happen among the vicious. It comes from the daily living out of the virtues, such as patience, charity, humility, as well as order and discipline, which ultimately creates the beautiful.

In 2005 the documentary *Into Great Silence* was released in Europe. It features the quiet but orderly life inside a Carthusian monastery high in the French Alps. To the surprise of everyone, it was a hit, winning many prestigious awards and viewed by millions more than expected. I recall being astounded to see it at the sales counters of many secular bookstores in Rome. The reason for its popularity was clearly not just its cinematography, but the quiet beauty revealed in daily monastic life—

something so many in our world are drawn to because of the constant noise and chaos that seem to surround us.

Living and Sharing Beauty, Truth, and Goodness

One night we had several friends visiting our home, including a very talented piano player. After dinner Luke sat down at the piano and played nearly every song we requested. Finally, as the evening was growing late and everyone was getting tired, I asked for one last song: "O God Beyond All Praising." Luke's wife had walked down the aisle to this hymn at their wedding, so he knew it well. One of our guests, Mr. Matheson, an eighty-year-old who had recently been widowed, had clearly been enjoying the evening with "the young people," as he called us. But as soon as Luke started in on the final hymn, the tears streamed down Mr. Matheson's face. I'm sure it was a combination of joy and sorrow, and missing his dear wife, for whom he had cared so diligently in the many years before her death. All his emotions were brought to the surface by the beauty and sublimity of the song. It was a small thing for Luke to entertain us, but I think his act of kindness reverberated in Mr. Matheson's soul much longer than it took for the song to be played.

John Paul was careful to remind us not to waste our efforts out of timidity or laziness. "Here we touch on an essential point. Those who perceive in themselves this kind of divine spark which is the artistic vocation—as poet, writer, sculptor, architect, musician, actor and so on—feel at the same time the obligation not to waste this talent but to develop it, in order to put it at the service of their neighbour and of humanity as a whole."[15] We have a sacred obligation to develop and share our talents. "Much will be required of the person entrusted with much, and still more will be demanded of the person entrusted with more" (Luke 12:48).

No matter what our talents, we must find ways not only to experience the beautiful, but to share it with others. It can be something as simple as singing carols at Christmas, playing the piano, discussing a book, visiting a museum, or sending a beautiful Christmas card. Even building a fire and watching the flames dance can re-ignite something in a soul. The idea is to remind the soul of the good, the true, and the beautiful and not to merely be distracted by the banalities of daily life.

And so we pray with Pope Benedict:

> *Let us hope that the Lord will help us to contemplate his beauty, both in nature as well as in works of art, so that we might be touched by the light of his face, and so also be light for our neighbor.*[16]

Eight

HOPE IN THE DARKNESS OF DEATH

Death is a very difficult topic in our culture, largely because we are so often removed from the process of it. Additionally, the emphasis upon eternal youth leaves many with the impression that they are invincible and will live forever. I heard one woman lament her deteriorating health: "Oh, why is this happening to me?" She was ninety years old!

Aside from the awkwardness of death in our culture, there is the reality of its finality. Often, particularly in the case of unexpected death, much is left unsaid and unfinished. All the things we plan to do down the road, or put off, assuming we have time to do them later, never get finished. Unfortunately many put their own spiritual preparation for death into this category. "This is not something to concern myself with today. Down the road," is the passing thought. And then the road gets shorter and shorter, and because we haven't established any sort of faith to rely upon, suddenly when the end comes, there is no foundation to stand on. Gratefully, for all of us God's mercy can fill in the gaps, if only we are open to it. Even when it looks like our best efforts have failed, there is always renewed hope in what God can do. At no point should we give up hoping or praying.

It Is Tough to Raise Good Parents

Edith, divorced and in her sixties, had lived a vibrant and adventurous life. She moved in with her daughter, Alison, who was a recent convert to the Catholic faith. One morning the three of us went for a walk after Mass. I remember thinking as we finished our hour together that there was no way Edith was going to convert. Her conversation had been riddled with New Age references, which I knew from my own upbringing in Oregon, and very secular ideals. Her own daughter had converted largely because of the overwhelming sense that something was missing in her life. But Edith, I thought, no way. And then several weeks later, Alison confided in me that her mother was joining the Church. After I picked my jaw up off the floor, all I could do was ask what had prompted it all. After years of searching for truth, Edith had found something firm to stand on.

The baby boomer generation is growing older. Many boomers are by and large un-churched or have long ago abandoned the faith of their youth. Their generation, as time grows shorter, urgently needs to hear the gospel message before it is too late. It is through their own children, often, that they hear the authentic and life-giving teachings of the Church. But how does a child—of any age—reach a parent? And what if that parent doesn't really act like a parent, but more like a teenager locked in a sixty- or seventy-year-old body? It has become a quip among many of my friends as they deal with their parents' alcoholism, divorces, awkward relationships, and heterodox views about faith that it is tough to raise good parents. Often it can be hard to discern who is the parent and who is the child on an emotional or spiritual level.

While it may seem that in many cases baby boomers have cornered the market on permanent adolescence, the one reassuring thing is that their hearts are not immune to conversion. Parents present their own challenges because there is usually a lot of baggage that has to be dealt with—decades of bad decisions, painful memories, and old wounds—and the wake that has followed their treacherous path. There also may be serious practical issues to sort out; for example, when someone is in a relationship that can't be reconciled to the faith. The one thing that is clear about conversions in people who are older is that God doesn't just clean up the surface issues, but goes much deeper, to authentic healing. A perfect novena, and a favorite of Pope Francis, is to Our Lady, Undoer of Knots. It may take time, but Our Lady goes deep to clear out the major issues impeding a soul of any age.

Deathbed Conversions

Near the end of Evelyn Waugh's novel *Brideshead Revisited*, the patriarch of the Marchmain family, who ran off to Italy with his mistress decades before, lies on his deathbed. As a lapsed Catholic he has objected to a priest coming to give him last rites in his final illness, though his children insist on bringing the priest to give him last rites after he's unconscious. Upon the completion of the sacrament, Lord Marchmain shockingly makes the Sign of the Cross, making it clear to all present that he has reconciled himself with God at death's door.

My own father passed away from pancreatic cancer in 1989. He had a strong faith and frequently received the sacraments. As his final hours approached, it had been several days since he had communicated anything to us; he was in a drug-induced coma. We knew the end was close and asked a priest to come and give him last rites. He lay in a hospital bed set up in our living room, appearing to be sleeping, as he had been for several days. The priest arrived, and as he started the sacrament with the Sign of the Cross, my father, like Lord Marchmain, made the sign with us. It was a powerful thing to see, particularly since it was the last gesture I would ever see him make. While his was nothing like a deathbed conversion, my point is that you never know what a soul hears or sees or feels when in a coma. Even if objections have been raised previously to having a priest present, it is never too late for grace to break in and transform a soul.

Many view deathbed conversion as a sign of weakness, although others have found its solace and reveled in a newfound joy and peace. Oscar Wilde, John Wayne, Gary Cooper, and Patricia Neal are among the most notable who have received this grace at the very end of their lives. Of course the most famous deathbed conversion was the Good Thief's as he was crucified next to Christ (Luke 23:39–42).

Karen Edmisten, in her book *Deathbed Conversions: Finding Faith at the Finish Line*, wrote of the experience of many who find their faith at death's door:

> *Living one's entire life without God, though, is hardly a free ticket. A true deathbed convert doesn't rub his hands together at the final hour, snickering, "Hey, I pulled a fast one on the Big Guy!" Rather, he sees the tragedy of a wasted lifetime, the pain of his prolonged denial, and the foolishness of his stubborn* Non Serviam. *The only glee is the relief and gratitude that God's mercy is offered and poured out to us until the final and bitter end.*[1]

One of the mysteries of life is that regardless of how well we know someone, we don't know what state a soul is in, or what grace may be doing for a particular soul. The Church has always strongly encouraged praying for the dying, particularly those who will die today. As we read in

Scripture, "Whoever sows sparingly will also reap sparingly; and whoever sows in bountifully will also reap bountifully" (2 Corinthians 9:6). As a result, many people die as they have lived, which should put all of us on alert. But God's grace and mercy are ever abundant. One nurse, who assisted those nearing death, wrote: "People grow a lot when they are faced with their own mortality. I learnt never to underestimate someone's capacity for growth. Some changes were phenomenal."[2]

When assisting those who are dying, aside from providing the invaluable sacraments of the Church, there are many things we can do to help them prepare. I have heard of doctors who, not wanting to upset a patient too much with the reality of the situation, are noncommittal about when death might come. Such efforts to help are truly a hindrance to what is called a "happy death." It is important for every soul, when possible, to have time to prepare for death. The recipe for a happy death includes reconciliation with family members and other close friends, both by offering and asking forgiveness, as well as by making peace with God and his Church. While putting material things in order can also be a source of great peace and consolation, the major focus should be upon relationships that cannot be sorted out after someone dies.

Susan Tassone, in her book *Prayers, Promises, and Devotions for the Holy Souls in Purgatory*, offers a very good list of prayers for the dying. Some of the basics include calling upon the saints for their divine assistance, especially Our Lady and St. Joseph, the patron saint of departing souls. There are also many promises associated with the Chaplet of Divine Mercy when the prayers are said for and by the dying. Sacramentals such as the scapular, holy water, relics, and the crucifix, can be helpful aids for those in their final distress. We can also ask a priest for the Apostolic Pardon or Apostolic Blessing when our loved one is near death. It is an indulgence for those who die in the state of grace, offering complete remission of all temporal punishment for sin.

Praying for the Dead

For decades Amanda prayed for her brother, Ryan, who, like his father before him, was an alcoholic. Both he and Amanda had watched their father slowly drink himself to death, and Ryan was following the same path. For years, as he married a beautiful woman, raised two children, and landed a good job, it seemed he could handle his drinking. And then, everything unraveled. His drinking went far beyond anything anyone could do for him. After yo-yoing through twelve-step programs and binge drinking, Ryan suffered his first stroke at forty years of age. It was after this stage that Amanda knew she needed to change the tack of her prayers. For decades her prayer had been for Ryan's healing, but now it was clear that he might not ever heal and she just needed to pray that he would be saved from hell. She prayed fervently for his salvation, even if it was to the lowest rung of purgatory. A few months after Amanda changed her prayer, Ryan died of a second stroke. His sister's only remaining hope was that her prayers had not left him defenseless in the hour of his death. For the rest of her life, Amanda will remember Ryan in her prayers, in hopes that he will one day make it into heaven.

Often at funerals—even most Catholic funerals—regardless of how a person lived his or her life, the deceased is somehow instantly transformed into a saint or an angel who has gone to a better place. While likely motivated by trying to preserve the memory of the deceased as well as make the best of a difficult situation, such canonizations are an incredible disservice to the soul who has died. It is this group of people attending the funeral, still living on earth, who have the greatest ability to pray the deceased out of purgatory and into heaven. And yet because they assume the deceased is already in heaven, no one prays for him or her.

Purgatory seems to be both very misunderstood and an undervalued mercy given to us by God. Heaven, the Church has always taught and the *Catechism* makes clear, is a place of spiritual perfection and purity. No one can be there who is not spiritually perfect. Hell, on the other hand, is for those who have separated themselves from God. But most of us won't fit into either category, so purgatory is the place that allows each of us to gain heaven despite our faults and failings. Otherwise, the next best option would truly condemn us to hell, given that heaven wouldn't be available to us.

The unique thing about purgatory, however, is that the soul who is there has no way to merit his own exit out and into heaven. His life is over, as are the opportunities to grow in loving God. It is only through the prayers and sacrifices of those on earth that a soul can be delivered into heaven.

The teachings on purgatory reach back to the Book of Maccabees in the Old Testament. The *Catechism of the Catholic Church* states,

> *From the beginning the Church has honored the memory of the dead and offered prayers in suffrage for them, above all the Eucharistic sacrifice, so that, thus purified, they may attain the beatific vision of God. The Church also commends almsgiving, indulgences, and works of penance undertaken on behalf of the dead.* (CCC, 1032)

These are the same sort of offerings recommended for the living, which shows the deep union between those on earth, those in purgatory anticipating heaven, and those already in heaven. Because of this interconnectedness, our prayers have the same effect as they would upon a soul still living on earth.

Ultimately, we should never despair that a soul has been lost to hell. We simply don't know, and we hope in the eternal mercy of our benevolent God and Father. Even in the case of suicide, the *Catechism* says,

> *We should not despair of the eternal salvation of persons who have taken their own lives. By ways known to him alone, God can provide the opportunity for salutary repentance. The Church prays for persons who have taken their own lives.* (CCC, 2283)

Our efforts to nudge those we love into heaven should continue even after death. It seems a tragedy to try to help them find God on earth but then to stop praying for them after they die, no matter how they lived their lives. Through our false canonizations, we abandon them to languish at the border of the promised land at the point when we can be their greatest help. A nudge from purgatory to heaven could be the greatest gift of all.

Tassone's book offers a wealth of information not only about how we can help the souls in purgatory, but about how they are anxious to help us. She includes the little-known practice of Gregorian Masses, in which Mass is said thirty consecutive days for the deceased. The practice was established by Pope Gregory the Great in the sixth century after he received a private revelation that his friend Justus had been delivered from purgatory on the thirtieth day of having Masses said for him. The book also includes a number of poignant prayers for the dead, particularly those who have died under tragic circumstances.

Ultimately, we will never know in this life what has been the final fate of a loved one. The best we can do is to forgive them, give them back to God, and remember that God loves them more than we do.

EPILOGUE

Not infrequently in our secular culture, we meet (and love) people whose lives appear to be devoid of God. Particularly if those people's lives don't appear to be in complete shambles, we can feel apprehensive that they might not really *need* God. The last thing we want to do is bother them with our personal faith. But whether they outwardly appear to need God our not, they really do. Don't let the absence of a crisis deceive you.

Pope Saint John Paul II, in his encyclical *Veritatis Splendor* (The Splendor of the Truth) speaks of the rich young man found in the Gospel of Matthew. This youth, who approaches Christ with a question about morality, the Polish pope makes clear, is not simply one individual who lived millennia ago, but he is us—every human being. He represents our search for meaning in this life; the fulfillment of our deepest desires; the quenching of our greatest longings. "This question," he explains, "is ultimately an appeal to the absolute Good which attracts us and beckons us; it is the echo of a call from God who is the origin and goal of man's life."[3] Christ is always the answer. And although we all may have the same question linger in our hearts, the ways to reach him are as unique as the person looking for him.

The truth is that we all need God. Like a fish that doesn't know he is in water, the water is still vital for his existence. The same is true of God and the tenets of the Church. Much like returning a child to his mother, evangelization is the restoration of the most fundamental of all relationships. What could be more natural than restoring the relationship between the Creator and his creature? While some are simply not in a place to hear it because of sin, more often than not, it is simply that people have never actually heard the truth. The more they hear, the more relevant it becomes as questions of identity and self-worth are answered; shallow interests give way to soaring wonder; a song of thanksgiving replaces curses of anger; self-absorption turns into a loving offering to meet the needs of others; and peace gently settles in where anxiety, insecurity, and shame once lived. What greater gift could you give to those you love? Do not be afraid to give it!

Our Lady of Guadalupe, *Pray for us.*

ACKNOWLEDGMENTS

Like most books, this one has been a labor of love, including the charity offered by others for its completion. I am grateful to the little parish of Stella Maris on Sullivan's Island, South Carolina, where the inspiration that led to this book was first sparked. I don't doubt that it is a fruit of the prayers for conversions said by the congregation after each Mass. I am also indebted to Heidi Hess Saxton who encouraged me to turn a short article into a book. Thank you, Matthew Kelly, for making this project a reality and to Kym Surridge for your diligent editing.

The witness of many friends and family populate the pages of these books. I'm grateful to you all for your courage, inspiration, faithfulness, and love.

And finally, I would like to thank my husband, Joseph, for all your editing suggestions, fine meals, and countless hours watching our children so I could work. This book would not exist without your love, patience, and encouragement.

BIOGRAPHY

Carrie Gress has a doctorate in philosophy from the Catholic University of America and was the Rome Bureau Chief of Zenit's English Edition. She is the co-author with George Weigel of *City of Saints: A Pilgrimage to John Paul II's Krakow* along with photographer Stephen Weigel (Image Books, 2015). A mother of four, she and her family live in Virginia.

END NOTES

Introduction

1. Austin Ivereigh, *The Great Reformer: Francis and the Making of a Radical Pope* (New York: Henry Holt and Company, 2015) 268.
2. Pope Francis, *The Joy of the Gospel: Evangelii Gaudium* (Erlanger, KY: The Dynamic Catholic Institute, 2014), 12.
3. Ibid.
4. Ibid., 22.
5. Austin Ruse, "The 7 Moments of My Conversion," Scribd, May 3, 2013, http://www.scribd.com/doc/197345996/The-7-Moments-of-My-Conversion-By-Austin-Ruse?fb_action_ids=10151861532331638&fb_action_types=og.likes&fb_source=other_multiline&action_object_map=[180647615478532]&action_type_map=[%22og.likes%22]&action_ref_map=[.
6. Pope Francis, *Evangelii Gaudium*, 10.
7. Pope Francis, *Evangelii Gaudium*, 288.

Chapter 1

1. Justin Taylor, "How Much Do You Have to Hate Somebody to Not Proselytize?" The Gospel Coalition, November 17, 2009, http://thegospelcoalition.org/blogs/justintaylor/2009/11/17/how-much-do-you-have-to-hate-somebody-to-not-proselytize/.
2. Saint Teresa of Avila, *The Collected Works of St. Teresa of Avila*, Volume 1, (Washington, DC: ICS Publications, 1987) Chapter 32.
3. Pope Francis, *Evangelii Gaudium*, 266.
4. Dwight Longenecker, "Talk About Wave Walking," Patheos, January 16, 2014, http://www.patheos.com/blogs/standingonmyhead/2014/01/talking-about-wave-walking.html.
5. "Pope Francis: Put Christian Words in Action," Vatican Radio, May 12, 2013, http://en.radiovaticana.va/storico/2013/12/05/pope_francis_put_christian_words_in_action/en1-752935.
6. Pope Francis, *Evangelii Gaudium*, 264.
7. Ibid., 91.
8. Ibid., 10.
9. Ibid., 9.
10. Ibid., 10.
11. Ibid., 1.

Chapter 2

1. Pope Francis, Evangelii Gaudium, 264.
2. Ibid.
3. Vatican II, *Dogmatic Constitution on the Church: Lumen Gentium* (Boston: Pauline Books and Media, 1965), 11.
4. Catherine Doherty, *How Christ Comes to Heal Us* (Madonna House Publications), Catholic Education Resource Center, 2012, http://www.catholiceducation.org/en/religion-and-philosophy/spiritual-life/how-christ-comes-to-heal-us.html.
5. Pope Francis, *Evangelii Gaudium*, 282.
6. Ibid.
7. Ibid., 283.

8. Ibid., 281.
9. Ibid., 283.

Chapter 3

1. Kevin Lowry, "You Want to Convert Me," Grateful Convert Blog, Oct. 2, 2013, http://gratefulconvert.com/you-want-to-convert-me/ .
2. Pope Francis, *Evangelii Gaudium*, 269.
3. Ibid.
4. Ibid., 288.
5. Ibid.
6. Ibid., 90.
7. Ibid., 88.
8. Ibid., 270.
9. David Clayton and Leila Marie Lawler, *The Little Oratory: A Beginner's Guide to Praying in the Home* (Manchester, NH: Sophia Institute Press, 2014), 15–16.
10. Pope Francis, *Evangelii Gaudium*, 85.
11. Ibid.
12. Ibid.

Chapter 4

1. http://whitelilyoftrinity.com/saints_quotes_suffering.html
2. Susan Tassone, *Prayers, Promises, and Devotions for the Holy Souls in Purgatory* (Huntington, IN: Our Sunday Visitor, 2012), 15–16.
3. Maria Faustina Kowalska, *Diary: Divine Mercy in My Soul* (Stockbridge, MA: Marian Press, 2005), 57.
4. Pope Francis, *Evangelii Gaudium*, 6.
5. Ibid.

Chapter 5

1. Pope Francis, *Evangelii Gaudium*, 127.
2. "A Tribute to Our Friend Tom O'Gorman," Focolare Movement, January 15, 2014, http://www focolare.org/ireland/news/2014/01/15/a-tribute-to-our-friend-tom-ogorman/.

Chapter 6

1. Pope Francis, *Evangelii Gaudium*, 90.
2. Ibid., 39.
3. Ibid., 41.
4. Ibid., 120.
5. Ibid., 21.
6. Ibid., 39.
7. Ibid., 21.
8. The Integrated Catholic Life, http://www.integratedcatholiclife.org/2011/01/daily-quote-from-st-ignatius-of-loyola-6/

Chapter 7

1. Sofia Cavalletti, *The Religious Potential of the Child: Experiencing Scripture and Liturgy with Young Children* (Chicago: Liturgy Training Publications, 1992)
2. Pope Francis, *Evangelii Gaudium*, 15.
3. Pope Benedict XVI, General Audience, (Vatican: The Holy See, Libreria Editrice Vaticana)Vatican Website. August 31, 2011.
4. Ibid.
5. Pope John Paul II, Letter to Artists (Vatican: The Holy See, Libreria Editrice Vaticana), Vatican Website, 1999, 16.
6. Ibid.
7. Pope Francis, *Evangelii Gaudium*, 167.
8. Karen Edmisten, Deathbed Conversions: Finding Faith at the Finish Line (Huntington, IN: Our Sunday Visitor, 2013), Kindle edition, chap. 9
9. Ibid., 167.
10. Pope Benedict XVI, General Audience.
11. Pope John Paul II, Letter to Artists, 5.
12. Pope John Paul II, Letter to Artists, 3
13. Saturday Night Live Transcipts, http://snltranscripts.jt.org/81/81aprose.phtml
14. Pope John Paul II, Letter to Artists, 3
15. Pope Benedict XVI. "The Way of Beauty." from On Beauty as a Way to God: Art "Is Like a Door Opened to the Infinite" (August 31, 2011).

Chapter 8

1. Edmisten, *Deathbed Conversions*, chap. 1.
2. Joe Martino, "The Top 5 Regrets of the Dying," Collective Evolution, April 27, 2013, http://www.collective-evolution.com/2013/04/27/the-top-5-regrets-of-the-dying/.
3. Pope John Paul II, *Veritatis Splendor* (Vatican: The Holy See, Libreria Editrice Vaticano) Vatican Website, August 6, 1993, 7